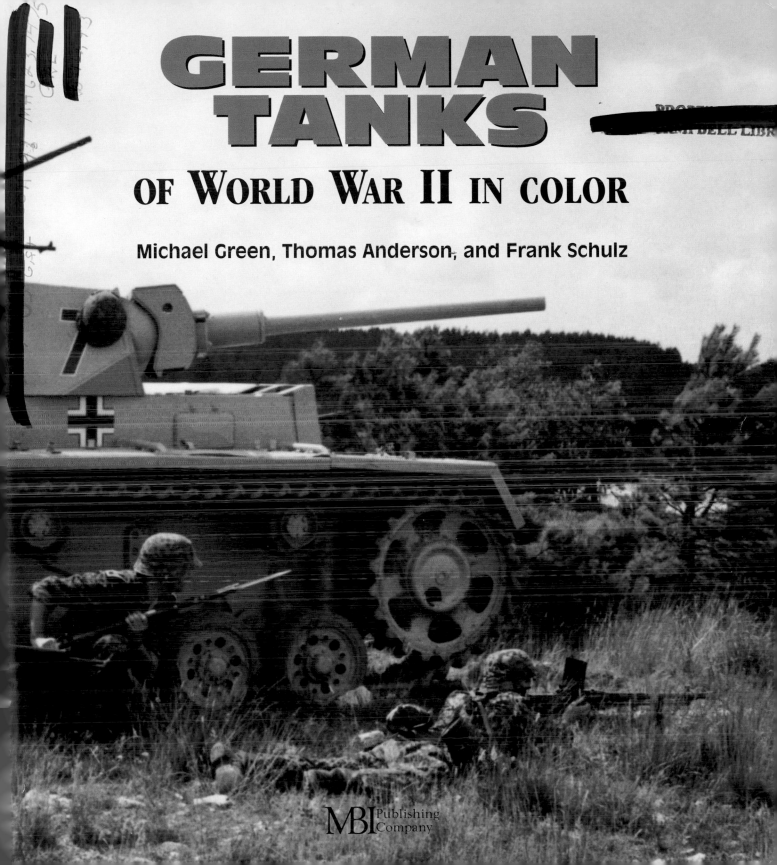

GERMAN TANKS
OF WORLD WAR II IN COLOR

Michael Green, Thomas Anderson, and Frank Schulz

MBI Publishing Company

To all the museum personnel and private collectors who have worked so hard
over the years to preserve the remaining examples of pre-1946 German military vehicles.

✦ ✦ ✦

First published in 2000 by MBI Publishing Company, 729 Prospect Avenue, PO Box 1, Osceola, WI 54020-0001 USA

MBI Publishing Company books are also available at discounts in bulk quantity for industrial or sales-promotional use. For details write to Special Sales Manager at Motorbooks International Wholesalers & Distributors, 729 Prospect Avenue, Osceola, WI 54020-0001 USA.

Library of Congress Cataloging-in-Publication Data
  Green, Michael.
    German tanks of World War II in color/Michael Green,
      Thomas Anderson & Frank Schulz.
        p. cm. —(Enthusiast color series)
    Includes index.
    ISBN 0-7603-0671-0 (pbk.: alk. paper)
    1. Tanks (Military science)—Germany. 2. World War, 1939–1945—Tank warfare. 3. Germany. Heer—Armored troops. I. Anderson, Thomas. II. Schulz, Frank. III. Title. IV. Series.
UG446.5.G687 2000
623.7'4752'094309044—dc21   99-052218

On the front cover: Seen in England at a 1997 military vehicle collector's show is this beautifully restored late-model Panzer III Ausf. L belonging to British collector Kevin Wheatcroft. *John Blackman*

On the frontispiece: A head-on shot of the Panzer IV Ausf. D belonging to the collection of the British Army Tank Museum shows the overhead hatches for the driver (on the right side of the superstructure) and the radio operator/machine gunner on his left. The front superstructure plate to the left of the driver's position is stepped back to improve his visibility. This feature was dispensed with in later production models of the Panzer IV. *British Army Tank Museum*

On the title page: The British Army Tank Museum's restored Panzer III Ausf. L is seen here posing with a number of history buffs in German World War II military uniforms during an annual open house event. *British Army Tank Museum*

On the back cover: Moved outside for display is a Jagdpanther turretless tank destroyer belonging to the British Army Tank Museum located in Southern England. The vehicle features a very late-war camouflage paint scheme applied by the museum staff. The paint scheme is based on a vehicle captured by the Canadian Army during the final weeks of the war in Europe. The vehicle has since been repainted in a more conventional German Army paint scheme generally known as the ambush pattern. *British Army Tank Museum*

Edited by Sara Perfetti

Designed by Jana Solberg

Printed in China

Contents

✦ ✦ ✦

ACKNOWLEDGMENTS

✦ ✦ ✦

Special thanks are due to the German Army Tank Museum, the Patton Museum of Cavalry and Armor, the British Army Tank Museum, the Wehrtechnische Studiensammlung (WTS), the U.S. Army Ordnance Museum, and the Japanese Ground Power Magazine. Individuals who made an extra effort in helping the authors include Dick Hunnicutt, George Bradford (editor of AFV News), Charles Lemons (Patton Museum curator), David Fletcher (British Army Tank Museum curator), and Dr. Jack Atwater (U.S. Army Ordnance Museum director). Additional help came from Ron Hare, Charles Kliment, Dean and Nancy Kleffman, Jacques Littlefield, Karl Vonder Linden, Richard Byrd, Bob Fleming, Andreas Kirchhoff, Richard Cox, Mert Wreford, and Richard Pemberton.

INTRODUCTION

✛ ✛ ✛

In September of 1916, in the middle of World War I, the British army hesitantly introduced the first crude tanks into combat. Only 32 of these slow and ungainly vehicles were fielded, and they failed to make much of an impression on the German army's high-ranking generals. However, a few farsighted German officers were alarmed enough by the new British invention to begin a tank development program of their own.

In the summer of 1917, less than one year after the British introduced their first tanks to the battlefield, the Germans began testing their first tank prototype. Influential German generals did not enthusiastically follow the tests. The subsequent failure of British tank operations in France only reinforced their belief that the new mechanical device was a novelty that had no future on the battlefield.

On November 20, 1917, the British army used more than 400 tanks in a successful attack against the German army. The top German generals then realized that a revolution in warfare had caught them by surprise. In response to the threat posed by the British army's sudden technical superiority, the German army quickly accelerated their tank development program, but German industry was unprepared for the rush orders and completed only 20 "A7V" tanks before the war came to an end.

On November 11, 1918, Germany agreed to an armistice that ended all fighting with the Allies. On June 28, 1919, the German government signed an official peace treaty with the Allies at Versailles, France. Under the terms of the Versailles Treaty, Germany was restricted to a small standing army of 100,000 men divided into seven infantry and four cavalry divisions. In addition, Germany was forbidden to possess tanks, heavy artillery, aircraft, submarines, and other offensive weapons.

Inspection teams (called Allied Control Commissions) were allowed free rein to monitor German compliance and enforce the weapons restrictions imposed by the Versailles Treaty. This did not stop the Germans. They continued to lay the groundwork for future generations of armored fighting vehicles, even though the last of the Allied Control Commissions were not withdrawn from Germany until early 1927.

By 1926 the German army had placed orders for a small number of experimental prototypes of turreted light and medium tanks. By 1928, with the cooperation of the Soviet government, the German army was testing these vehicles at a Russian military base 450 miles east of Moscow. German officers were also instructed on the theory of commanding tanks. The secret arrangements with the Russians allowed the Germans to proceed with their tank development program without alarming France or England. The Russians had minimal experience in developing their own tanks and were keen to acquire the Germans' technology. In 1934, when the Germans had no further use for Russian cooperation, they terminated the secret agreements.

In step with their interest in the development of tank technology, the German army took a great deal of interest in the progressive work done by the British army in the 1920s and early 1930s on

Anatomy of a Tank

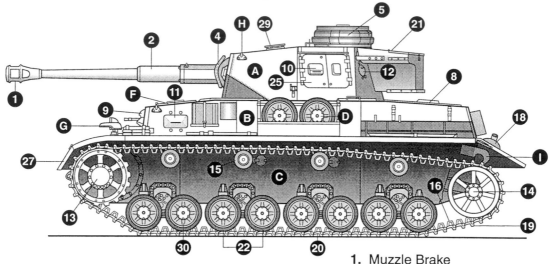

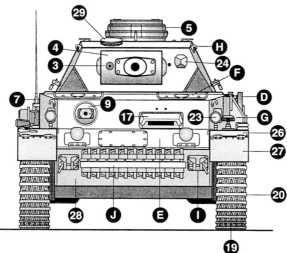

1. Muzzle Brake
2. Main Armament, Gun Barrel, Tube
3. Coaxial Machine Gun
4. Mantlet, Mantle
5. Commander's Cupola
6. Cupola Hatch
7. Aerial, Antenna & Mount
8. Engine Deck
9. Bow Machine Gun
10. Turret View Port
11. Hull View Port
12. Pistol Port
13. Front Drive Sprocket
14. Rear Idler Wheel
15. Return Roller
16. Track Guide Teeth
17. Driver's Vision Port
18. Exhaust, Muffler
19. Tracks
20. Track Links, Treads, Shoes
21. Turret Stowage Bin
22. Bogie Suspension Unit
23. Headlight
24. Front View Port
25. Turret Side Hatch Doors
26. Fender
27. Fender Flap
28. Front Bow Plate
29. Turret Roof Vent
30. Bogie Wheel

A. Turret
B. Upper Hull
C. Lower Hull
D. Spare Wheel
E. Glacis Plate
F. Driver's Hatch
G. Notek Night Light
H. Lift Hook
I. Tow Hooks
J. Spare Tracks

both the practical and theoretical employment of tanks. The German army replicated British experiments with tanks and tank tactics, including the use of radios for command and control. The results of these experiments, and others devised by the Germans, were used to plan the first tank battles.

The German army used mock-up Panzers (tanks) on civilian vehicle chassis during training exercises. This gave the Germans valuable experience in the handling of large formations of military vehicles, while still adhering to the precise terms of the hated Versailles Treaty.

The Nazi Party, under the leadership of Adolf Hitler, took over the German government in January of 1933, which set the stage for the German army, led by its embryonic tank force, to become the world's most feared military force within the span of a few years.

Despite its fearsome reputation, the German army never had as many tanks as it needed in World War II. Tank units never made up more than 20 percent of the total number of divisions in the German army. Throughout World War II, the German army remained primarily an infantry force that marched into battle on its feet. There were a number of reasons for this. One of the most crucial was the fact that German factories just did not have the manufacturing capability or trained labor force to meet the demands placed upon them by Hitler's military adventures. In early 1939 German industrial leaders estimated it would be at least several more years before they could build up their capacity to support the needs of their military forces.

This book will attempt to cover the history of German tanks (including foreign tanks in German service) from roughly 1932 through the end of World War II. It was during this time span that the German army developed and fielded some of the most famous tanks in the history of ground warfare.

This work is a very broad overview of the subject. There is plenty of material for many more volumes devoted to the subject. Those readers interested in studying German tanks in more detail will find the selected bibliography at the back of the book useful.

We have included selected color photographs of preserved German tanks and other armored vehicles to illustrate the text. Some of the vehicles pictured have been lovingly restored to near-original condition by dedicated museum staff and volunteers. Private collectors have carefully restored others. Still others (as can clearly be seen in some of our pictures) have suffered from years of neglect.

The photographs in this book vary in condition because of the different ages of the film used. Some of the original film negatives are 50 years old. The authors have decided to include some photographs with marginal color quality to depict historic German army paint schemes, or German vehicles no longer on display.

Where color photographs of interesting German vehicles are not available, the authors have relied upon color artwork and line drawings from George Bradford.

Color photographs similar to those in this book can be purchased from Panzer Prints, The Falcon, Leverton Road, Sturton le Steeple, Retford, Notts DN22 9HE, England. Color prints of German tanks and other vehicles can also be ordered from the British Army Tank Museum, Bovington Camp, Wareham, Dorset BH20 6JG, England, or from the museum's Web site (www.tankmuseum.co.uk). Line drawings can be purchased from George Bradford, R.R. 32, Cambridge, Ontario, Canada N3H 4R7 or from his Web site (www.steelchariots.net/bradford.htm).

One

LIGHT TANKS

✦ ✦ ✦

In the late 1920s, the German army decided that the optimal choice for their future armored force was a medium tank (15 to 20 tons) with a five-man crew. They felt that smaller light tanks were too limited in the armament they could carry, crew size, and armor protection. Unfortunately, the industrial infrastructure of the country was incapable of producing the requisite number of medium tanks at that time.

A compromise position was taken at the highest levels of the German army. As an interim measure, the German army planned for a fleet of small light training tanks. The ordnance department of the German army issued a requirement in 1932 for the design of a simple and inexpensive vehicle weighing about 5 tons.

Krupp, Henschel, Daimler-Benz, Maschinenfabrik Augsburg-Nurnberg (MAN), and other German industrial firms submitted design proposals for the army's evaluation. Krupp's light tank design was chosen by the German army, but Henschel won the manufacturing contract.

On the move during an event marking the 10th anniversary of the founding of the German Army Tank Museum is a Panzer I Ausf. B commanded by World War II panzer veteran Kurt Fischer. The tank is painted in panzer gray with white national markings to duplicate a vehicle that would have taken part in the invasion of Poland in September 1939. The vehicle was found buried in the ground in southern Germany in 1984. *Thomas Anderson*

As the prime contractor and system integrator, Henschel was responsible for coordinating a variety of suppliers for the components needed to assemble the vehicle. The company began testing prototypes (hand-tooled examples of a final product) in early 1934. Low-rate production of the new Pz.Kpfw. I Ausfuehrung A light tank began in July 1934.

The designation *Pz.Kpfw.* is an abbreviation for *Panzerkampfwagen*, which translates into English as an armored fighting vehicle (AFV), or tank. The designation *Pz.Kpfw.* was always followed by a Roman numeral to indicate the basic configuration, or type. Within the German army the term *Panzerkampfwagen* was commonly shortened to *Panzer* or just the letters *Pz.*

A Panzer I Ausf. B currently on display at the U.S. Army Ordnance Museum at Aberdeen Proving Ground, Maryland. The Ausf. B version of the Panzer I was first issued to German tank units in 1935. Like all German tanks produced between 1932 and 1945, the vehicle has an all-steel track. Until recently, the vehicles belonging to the Ordnance Museum collection were repainted with little regard to historical accuracy. *Michael Green*

The term *Ausfuehrung* shortened to *Ausf.* and followed by a capital letter indicates the version of a tank referred to in conversation or in written reports. Model differences between tanks in the same series can reflect changes in performance, standard equipment, production techniques, or improvements based on field experience. These differences can reflect both internal and external changes to a particular production run of a vehicle. Not all versions of a particular tank reach full-scale production owing to unavailability of critical materials, failure to meet required performance, high cost, or changes in military tactics.

During World War II the Germans rebuilt worn out or damaged tanks with components

This picture of the Panzer I Ausf. B belonging to the German Army Tank Museum shows the various details on the front of the vehicle including towing cable, lights, vision ports, and shovel. The small turret on the Panzer I is slightly offset to the left of the superstructure. World War II panzer veteran Kurt Fischer restored the vehicle's hull and transmission in his farmyard. *Thomas Anderson*

from different production runs of the same vehicle. This can make positive identification of a German tank very difficult at times.

The British army (and later, the American army) substituted the designation *Mark* or *Mk.* for *Panzerkampfwagen,* using the German's Roman numeral designation to identify the different types of German tanks. This form of identification is commonly found in English language publications on the subject, and it will appear in various reports and quotes found in this book.

PANZER I

The 818 Panzer I Ausf. A tanks built between July 1934 and June 1936 were 13 feet 3 inches long, 6 feet 9 inches wide, and only 5 feet 8 inches

This small armored command version of the Panzer I belonging to the British Army Tank Museum features a light green paint scheme and markings duplicating a vehicle used by the German army's 21st Panzer Division in North Africa. Armament for the vehicle consisted of a single 7.92-mm machine gun in the front of the superstructure. *British Army Tank Museum*

tall. Reflecting its design origins as an interim light tank, the Panzer I Ausf. A had only 13 millimeters of steel armor protection. This armor protected the two-man crew (driver and vehicle commander) from small-arms fire only. The crew communicated with each other through a voice tube.

Armament on the Panzer I Ausf. A consisted of two 7.92-mm machine guns. The vehicle carried a maximum of 1,525 rounds. The side-by-side machine guns were mounted in a small hand-operated rotating turret. The vehicle commander acted as the gunner and sat on a seat suspended from the turret that rotated with the turret as it turned.

Power for the Panzer I Ausf. A came from a four-cylinder air-cooled Krupp gasoline engine and was geared for a top speed of 23 miles per hour. Standardizing gasoline engines was a pre-war decision made by the German army based on the advice of the German liquid-fuels industry. The tank carried enough fuel for a maximum range of 125 miles. In common with all German tanks, the transmission was at the front of the hull. (The hull is the part of a tank that contains the crew, engine, transmission, and all associated equipment.)

The suspension system on the proposed Krupp design was copied from a small British light tank known as the Carden Lloyd Mark VI. This field-proven suspension concept was a major reason Krupp won the design competition. The German military knew that it would minimize the potential performance and schedule risks of developing a vehicle-specific suspension system.

A Panzerjaeger (tank hunter) I in a paint scheme used in North Africa. The Panzerjaeger I was the German army's first tank destroyer. The Czech 47-mm antitank gun mounted on the vehicle was far superior to anything the Germans had in the early part of the war. The Panzerjaeger I two-man gun crew had access to 86 rounds of ammunition within the vehicle. *George Bradford*

Within the British Army Tank Museum's vast collection of armored fighting vehicles from around the world is this Panzer II Ausf. F. The vehicle is shown in an early World War II panzer gray paint scheme as would have been seen during the invasion of France in May 1940. This version of the Panzer II first entered field service in early 1941. It featured increased armor protection over earlier versions. *British Army Tank Museum*

The suspension system put into production by Henschel consisted of two suspension assemblies per side. Each suspension assembly consisted of a walking beam fitted with two bogie wheels that rode on the top of the steel track. The bogie assemblies of the Panzer I Ausf. A were attached to the hull by bolts and quarter-elliptic leaf springs. Three track return rollers were mounted on either side of the hull. The drive sprockets were at the front of the hull. The prominent rear idler wheels were adjustable fore and aft to set track tension.

Sustained high cross-country speeds caused overheating of the Krupp air-cooled engine. A decision was made to lengthen the vehicle's chassis to accommodate a larger, more powerful, water-cooled six-cylinder Maybach engine. Vehicles with the new engine configuration were designated Panzer I Ausf. B. Subsequent to this change, all German tanks were powered by Maybach water-cooled gasoline engines of various types and sizes.

A total of 675 Ausf. B vehicles were produced between August 1935 and June 1937. Work was also proceeding on Ausf. C and Ausf. D versions of the Panzer I during this period. The Ausf. C never passed the prototype stage, while 40 of the Ausf. D versions were built and fielded between

This beautifully preserved example of a Panzer II Ausf. G belongs to the German Army Tank Museum at Munster. It was acquired on long-term loan from the U.S. Army Ordnance Museum in 1989. The German museum staff painted the vehicle in a sand-colored scheme similar to what it might have worn in North Africa. The ammunition for the tank's 20-mm gun came in 10-round magazines, of which the vehicle carried 18. *Thomas Anderson*

July and December of 1942 before production was canceled.

Panzer I light tanks played a prominent role in the German invasions of Poland in September 1939, and of France in May 1940. Aware of the vehicle's marginal battlefield performance, the Germans were not surprised by the high losses suffered in both campaigns. Because they lacked anything better, the Germans also employed Panzer I light tanks in the early stages of the invasion of the Soviet Union and the battles with the British army in North Africa.

SELECTED PANZER I VARIANTS

The Germans often modified production tanks to serve specific purposes. This cost-effective method of using an existing chassis is practiced to this day by all industrial nations.

The best-known variant of the Panzer I was a small armored command vehicle based on the chassis of the Ausf. A and Ausf. B. The Panzer I command variant replaced the turret with a box-like armored superstructure housing the three-man crew and two long-range radios. (The superstructure of a tank is that part of the hull rising above the level of the tracks.) Between 1935 and 1937 a total of 184 Panzer I command vehicles rolled off German production lines.

The German army produced its first stopgap tank destroyer in 1939. It used the Panzer I Ausf. B chassis. This variant, generally known as the Panzerjaeger I, carried a 47-mm Czech gun. The Panzerjaeger (tank hunter) had a three-man crew and carried 86 rounds of ammunition.

On the move during a 1993 event marking the 10th anniversary of the founding of the German Army Tank Museum at Munster is a Panzer II Ausf. G belonging to the museum's collection. Clearly visible is the vehicle's suspension system with its front drive sprocket, rear idler wheel, and five bogie wheels. Above the road wheels are the track return rollers. At the rear of the vehicle's turret is a stowage bin. *Thomas Anderson*

THE ORGANIZATION AND ROLE OF THE PANZER DIVISION

The first three German army panzer divisions were formed in 1935 with a target goal of 561 tanks in each division. Due to the shortage of tanks, this goal was never met. Even if this number had been available, 561 tanks was seen by senior German officers as an unmanagable number and was soon decreased.

By 1939, shortly before the German invasion of Poland, the German army had six panzer divisions with a total strength on paper of 400 light and medium tanks each. This figure also proved unreachable and was revised downward during the winter of 1940 to approximately 200 tanks in each panzer division. In reality, even this figure was seldom met.

In the fall of 1943, the German army issued a new table of organization calling once again for a total of at least 200 tanks in each of its panzer divisions. This planned strength also proved unrealistic. Even the most elite panzer divisions in the German army typically contained no more than 150 tanks. Most panzer divisions had only 100 tanks at any given time. The German army's inability to replace its losses quickly resulted in panzer divisions with no more than a couple dozen tanks.

Because of their political status with Hitler, the Waffen-SS panzer divisions tended to get first crack at new tank production. This allowed them to have a full complement of tanks rarely seen in their army counterparts.

This rare old photo of a Luchs (Lynx) armored reconnaissance vehicle at Aberdeen Proving Ground, Maryland, shortly after the end of World War II is important because the vehicle is in its original camouflage colors. Due to a lack of interest by the U.S. Army in preserving the vehicle, it was cut up during a Korean War scrap drive. *Charles Kliment collection*

The Panzerjaeger I was too small, and the gun too large, to fit within the confines of a rotating armored turret. The gun was placed in a limited-traverse mount on top of the vehicle. This arrangement required that the vehicle be turned toward the direction of its target. Thin, flat, steel-armored plates on the front and sides of the weapon gave the gun crew limited protection from small-arms fire and artillery fragments.

The Panzerjaeger I first saw action during the invasion of France in May 1940. It would also be used in North Africa and during the beginning stages of the German invasion of the Soviet Union in June 1941. It was pulled from service in late 1941.

A high-ranking German officer in World War II wrote an article in a postwar American military magazine discussing the theoretic tactical employment of Panzerjaegers versus wartime battlefield reality. In that 1953 article, the author described how in theory Panzerjaegers were held in reserve until a threat appeared. Once enemy tanks were spotted, the Panzerjaegers would rush forward into previously reconnoitered concealed positions. Here, they would await the enemy tanks.

In practice, the high silhouette of the Panzerjaegers and their thin armor protection made the theoretic tactical employment of Panzerjaegers very difficult to implement. Due to their height, the vehicles often could not find suitable concealed firing positions. Compounding the problem was the fact that Soviet tank units normally preferred open terrain for their attacks. So, the Panzerjaegers were often forced to take up firing positions that, despite the attempts to camouflage them, could not be kept hidden from the enemy. Hence, they swiftly fell prey to hostile tanks or artillery fire.

Another problem faced on the eastern front by Panzerjaegers was the fact that Soviet tanks often appeared suddenly, without warning. When they did appear, their tendency was to punch through German defensive positions without pause and drive deep into the rear areas.

On display at the British Army Tank Museum is this Luchs (Lynx) armored reconnaissance vehicle that was captured in France by British army units shortly after the D-Day landings in Normandy in June 1944. The Lynx weighed a little less than 12 tons and featured the same turret-mounted 20-mm gun with a coaxial 7.92-mm machine gun as the standard Panzer II light tank. *British Army Tank Museum*

This made it impossible for the Panzerjaegers to reach their carefully reconnoitered firing positions in time. They were thus forced to take up battle while still on the move. In this type of battlefield situation their lack of a 360-degree rotating turret, and thin armor, left them hopelessly outclassed by the enemy tanks.

Despite these shortcomings, the Panzerjaegers successfully filled the gap until better-designed vehicles called Jagdpanzers could take their place. As the German army began fielding more of the better-designed Jagdpanzers, the production of Panzerjaegers decreased.

PANZER II

In July of 1934, the German army issued a set of requirements for a light tank weighing about 10 tons. It had hoped to field a larger and more useful medium tank, but serious production problems removed this plan from consideration. The new light tank was designated Panzer II.

This 1970s-era picture shows a Marder II Panzerjaeger (tank destroyer) on display outside the Patton Museum of Cavalry and Armor at Fort Knox, Kentucky. To preserve the vehicle from the elements, it has been in long-term interior storage since the 1980s. The camouflage scheme seen on the vehicle is not original but only a re-creation by the museum staff. *Dean and Nancy Kleffman*

The first prototype version of the Panzer II built by Henschel weighed 7.2 tons. Like most tank designs it would grow in weight as the design matured. The Panzer II three-man crew consisted of a driver in the front of the hull, and the vehicle commander and loader in the 360-degree rotating turret. A voice tube provided communication between the vehicle commander and the driver. The vehicle commander sat on a seat affixed to the turret while the loader stood on the floor of the turret basket.

Because of the very small size of the vehicle, the crew members of the Panzer II had dual roles. The loader also acted as the radio operator, and the vehicle commander also served as the gunner. The dual role of the tank commander/gunner was common to many other tanks of the day. The British army, and later the German army, realized early on that saddling the vehicle commanders with the extra duties of a gunner was distracting them from the more important duties of commanding the tanks and coordinating with other vehicles on the battlefield. This fault would be rectified on German tanks with the introduction of larger medium tanks, because a third man was added to the turret.

The armament of the Panzer II consisted of a turret-mounted 20-mm gun and a single coaxial 7.92-mm machine gun. The 360-degree rotating turret was turned by hand using a traverse

On display at the U.S. Army Ordnance Museum is this Czech-designed and built light tank known in German army service as the Panzer 35(t). This vehicle was the most numerous one in the Czech army when German forces seized the country in March 1939. In Czech service, the vehicle was designed for a crew of only three men. Once taken into German army service the vehicle received a fourth crewman. *Michael Green*

wheel. There was storage space for 180 rounds of 20-mm ammunition and 2,550 rounds of 7.92-mm ammunition.

The first four versions of the Panzer II retained the same type of suspension system as fitted to the Panzer I. The only difference was

the addition of an extra bogie wheel on either side of the vehicle's hull, making the Panzer II 2 feet 4 inches longer than the Panzer I.

To prevent expensive and time-consuming correction of inevitable problems during production, most vehicle programs enter an LRIP (Low

On display at the U.S. Army Ordnance Museum is a Marder III. This vehicle was a stopgap effort by the German army to place an anti-tank gun powerful enough to deal with the Soviet army's T-34 medium tank on the chassis of the Panzer 38(t). The vehicle was very successful in its intended role despite it poor armor protection. Of the 365 units built, the great majority were sent to the eastern front to fight the Soviet army. *Michael Green*

Rate Initial Production) phase prior to full-scale production. The Panzer II was no exception.

The LRIP version of the Panzer II was designated Ausf. c and entered LRIP in 1936. The vehicle sported a new German-designed suspension system better suited to the increased weight of the vehicle. It consisted of five slightly larger bogie wheels attached to quarter-elliptical leaf springs.

The success of the Ausf. c LRIP version of the Panzer II led to approval for volume production. MAN and other German firms started high-rate production in July of 1937. The production version was designated Panzer II Ausf. A. Minor

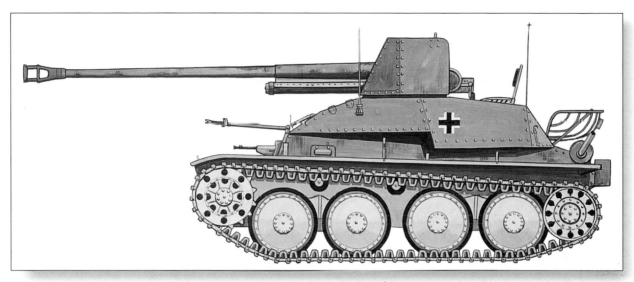

A Marder III as it appeared in North Africa with General Erwin Rommel's famous Afrika Korps. Sixty-six of these vehicles were shipped to Africa between July and November 1942. The Marder III was 15 feet 3.1 inches long, 7 feet 8.5 inches wide, and 8 feet 1.6 inches tall. The powerful 76.2-mm gun could easily punch holes in most enemy tanks. The vehicle was also equipped with a 7.92-mm machine gun for protection from enemy infantry. *George Bradford*

improvements to the Ausf. A production version that included a cupola (a small, one-man armored superstructure containing vision devices, which sits on top of the turret of the tank and allows the vehicle commander to observe what is going on around the tank without exposing his upper body to enemy fire) was designated Panzer II Ausf. B. This was followed in turn by the Ausf. C production version. The Ausf. A, B, and C versions of the Panzer II had extra angled armor added to the front of the vehicle's hull. German industry built 1,113 examples of the Ausf. c, A, B, and C versions of the Panzer II between March 1937 and April 1940.

The Panzer II Ausf. D and E versions were very similar to the Panzer II Ausf. C except for the suspension system employed. Versions D and E used an unusual suspension system consisting of four large road wheels on either side of the hull. The road wheels were attached to torsion bars anchored to the hull at the side opposite the road wheel. (Torsion bars are long steel rods that act as torsional springs. A bearing at the road wheel end allows free rotation; the far end is anchored to the hull so it cannot rotate.)

The new suspension gave the vehicle a top off-road speed of 36 miles per hour. There was no need for return rollers because the track was supported by the large road wheels. Only 43 examples of the Panzer II Ausf. D and E versions were built, between May 1938 and August 1939.

The Germans learned from combat experience that they needed to increase the armor protection on the Panzer II Ausf. C from 30 millimeters to 35 millimeters. This up-armored version was called Ausf. F and entered service in early 1941. The added armor increased the weight of the vehicle to 9.35 tons and, as expected, resulted in lower vehicle agility and top vehicle speed. German documents indicate that the vehicle's top speed dropped to 15 miles per hour with the added armor weight. This extra armor still did not adequately protect the Ausf. F on the battlefield. Nonetheless, German industry fielded 524

A Marder III Ausf. M on display at the U.S. Army Ordnance Museum. It represents a design improvement over the earlier Marder III. This was accomplished by moving the main gun from the center of the Czech 38(t) chassis to the rear of the vehicle, allowing the frontal armor plate on the vehicle's hull to slope at a better angle to deflect enemy weapons. It also improved access to the main armament by the gun crew. *Michael Green*

Panzer II Ausf. F vehicles between March 1941 and December 1942.

By the time Germany invaded France in May 1941, Panzer II light tanks were seriously outmatched by French tanks with their larger guns, better armor protection, and higher mobility. Superior battlefield tactics and a highly motivated organization prevented the total destruction of the Panzer II and the older Panzer I force. The Panzer II was also employed in North Africa and the Soviet Union as a reconnaissance vehicle before being pulled from front-line service.

SELECTED PANZER II VARIANTS

In 1939, acknowledging the limitations of the first production Panzer II units, the German army issued a set of requirements for a special Panzer II reconnaissance version. The results appeared on the battlefield in 1943 as the Panzer II Ausf. L. This designation was later changed to Luchs (Lynx). The vehicle weighed 11.8 tons and had a crew of four men.

The suspension system on the Lynx consisted of five large overlapping road wheels on either side of the hull. The axle for each wheel was mounted to the end of a roadarm. Each roadarm rotated around a bearing at the hull end. A torsional spring (torsion bar) rigidly attached to the hull on the opposite side of the vehicle provided independent springing for the suspension. The improved suspension, coupled with a Maybach six-cylinder 180-horsepower engine, gave the Lynx a top speed of 38 miles per hour. The Lynx retained the standard

Panzer II armament—a 20-mm main gun and a coaxial 7.92-mm machine gun. A few of the 111 units built had a 50-mm gun fitted. Production of the Lynx ended in January 1944.

The Panzerjaeger variants of the Panzer II Ausf. A, B, C, and F were fitted with a limited-traverse 75-mm gun. A three-sided thin armored superstructure, open at the top and rear, protected the three-man gun crew. In this configuration, the vehicle was commonly known as the Marder II. German industry constructed 201 examples of the vehicle between April 1942 and June 1943. The Marder II would remain in use with the German military until Germany's surrender.

SELECTED FOREIGN LIGHT TANKS IN GERMAN SERVICE

Prior to the armed German takeover of Poland in September 1939, Hitler managed the peaceful takeovers of Austria and Czechoslovakia. With his possession of Czechoslovakia, Hitler acquired a thriving and capable arms industry. Among the many items of military hardware designed and produced by the Czech factories were a couple of fairly advanced light tanks, both of which were quickly introduced into German military service. The importance of these foreign-made vehicles is clearly evident in the fact that, of the 17 German panzer divisions involved in the initial invasion of the Soviet Union in June

Seen here at Aberdeen Proving Ground shortly after World War II is a Grille (Cricket) self-propelled howitzer. This picture is very rare since it shows the vehicle's original camouflage scheme when it arrived in the United States. Like the Marder III Panzerjaeger (tank destroyer), it was based on the chassis of the Panzer 38(t). The vehicle's three-man gun crew had access to 18 rounds within the vehicle. *Charles Kliment collection*

1941, six were equipped mainly with Czech-made tanks.

The Czech light tanks that entered German service were the LTvz. 35 and the LTvz. 38. Both weighed about 10 tons and were powered by gasoline engines. Armament on both vehicles consisted of a 37-mm high-velocity antitank gun and two 7.92-mm machine guns. Armor protection on the vehicles ranged from 8-mm to 25-mm steel plates. Unlike the more advanced welded steel armor construction of German tanks, the Czech tanks used bolts to attach armor plates to a separate steel structural frame.

The LTvz. 35 first entered Czech army service in 1937. With their takeover of Czechoslovakia, the Germans acquired 244 LTvz. 35 light tanks. As the Panzer 35(t), it took part in the German invasions of France in May 1940 and the Soviet Union in June 1941. In 1942, the Germans pulled the vehicle from front-line use, unhappy with some of its design features. Thereafter, only a few turretless vehicles would be employed as towing vehicles.

The LTvz. 38 had been the winner of a competition for a new light tank for the Czech army in 1938. Only 10 of the vehicles had been completed when the German army took control of the country. They were soon placed into German army service with the designation Panzer 38(t).

The Panzer 38(t) suspension system consisted of eight large bogie wheels, four on either side of the hull. As with its German light tank counterparts, the drive sprockets were at the front of the vehicle with the idler wheels at the rear.

The Germans were quick to appreciate the outstanding design features of the Panzer 38(t) and ordered its continued production in May 1939. It would remain in production under German supervision until October 1941, with more than 1,400 units built. The Panzer 38(t) saw service in the German army during the invasions of Poland, France, and the Soviet Union before it was classified as an obsolete gun-armed tank.

The Germans used the Panzer 38(t) chassis for a wide range of different battlefield roles. One

In this picture taken at Aberdeen Proving Ground shortly after World War II is a Hetzer (Hunting Dog) in its original wartime scheme. The Hetzer was the German army's first purpose-built Jadgpanzer (tank destroyer). It was designed to replace the tall and poorly protected Marder III Panzerjaeger as well as the improved Ausf. H and M versions. *Charles Kliment collection*

of the best known gun armed conversions was the light tank destroyer called Panzerjaeger 38(t).

The Panzerjaeger 38(t), also called the Marder III, was fitted with a captured Soviet 76.2-mm gun in a limited-traverse mount. The enemy gun was merely placed on the open topped Panzer 38(t) chassis and protected by a thin, three-sided armored superstructure. This was the same arrangement found on the German conversion of the obsolete Panzer II into the Marder II.

Within a short time span the Germans put 383 units of the Panzerjaeger 38(t) into service. When the supply of captured Soviet guns ran short, the Germans further modified the chassis to accept their own 75-mm antitank gun. This configuration was designated Panzerjaeger 38(t) Ausf. H. German industry produced 275 units between November 1942 and April 1943.

Unhappy with the placement of the anti-tank guns on the first two versions of the

This picture, taken during a World War II historical reenactment display, shows a Hetzer featuring late-war camouflage colors. This vehicle, like so many others currently seen in museums and private collections, once served as a Swiss army vehicle. Switzerland acquired 158 of these former German army vehicles from the Czech government shortly after World War II ended. When the Swiss army no longer had a need for these vehicles, they were given to interested parties willing to pay the transportation charges. *Richard Pemberton*

Panzerjaeger 38(t), the Germans moved the power pack to the front of the hull. This allowed the gun to be placed at the rear of the vehicle for better crew access. Production of the revised vehicle—now designated Panzerjaeger 38(t) Ausf. M—started in April 1943 and ended in May 1944 with a total of 942 units built.

Another well-known variant, the Jagdpanzer 38(t), is better known by its unofficial nickname, the Hetzer (Hunting Dog). The Hetzer was a major modification of the 38(t), replacing the entire superstructure. As a purpose-built tank destroyer, it boasted a low-slung, well-sloped armored superstructure that supported a four-man crew and a 75-mm gun. This powerful gun could destroy almost all enemy tanks it might encounter. A roof-mounted, 7.92-mm remote-control machine gun served as the secondary armament.

Due to its excellent mobility and low height (6 feet, 10.7 inches), the Hetzer was a difficult target for enemy tanks. Its combination of firepower, armor, and mobility made it highly demanded by the German military in the last two years of the war. However, Hetzer crews disliked the vehicle's limited-traverse main gun and the cramped and awkwardly arranged crew stations. Czech factories produced 3,019 Hetzers between April 1944 and May 1945.

The chassis of the Panzer 38(t) was also modified to accept a 150-mm howitzer in a limited-traverse mount. In this configuration, the vehicle was commonly known as the Grille (Cricket). There were two versions of the Cricket, designated Ausf. H and Ausf. K. The main difference between the two versions was the location of the weapon. The weapon was mounted near the center of the hull in the rear-engine Ausf. H. The front-engine Ausf. K allowed mounting of the howitzer at the rear of the hull. In both versions, the gun crew was protected on the front and sides by an open-topped, thin-armor steel superstructure. Czech factories, under German control, constructed a total of 392 Grilles between February 1943 and September 1944.

After the successful invasion of France in May 1940, the German army had control of the French army tanks. Due to various design faults, including one-man turrets, the Germans considered the French vehicles generally unsuitable for front-line service and banished them to rear area security missions.

One of the French tanks to see service with the German army was the Hotchkiss H-35 light tank. It was a two-man tank powered by a gasoline engine and armed with a turret-mounted 37-mm antitank gun. The German army acquired over 800 Hotchkiss H-35s and placed them into service as the Panzer 38H 735(f).

In open storage at the Bulgaria Army Museum is this Hotchkiss H-35 French army light tank. In German army service the two-man vehicle was designated the Panzer 38H and used in rear area security duties. Armor protection on the vehicle was 40 millimeters at its thickest, far better than found on its German light tank counterparts in 1939. *Thomas Anderson*

Two

MEDIUM TANKS

✦ ✦ ✦

In 1934, having gained valuable experience with the early design work on the Panzer I, and after long debate about the types of tanks needed, the German army issued design requirements for a new medium tank. The tank was to have a five-man crew and weigh less than 24 tons. Armament was to consist of a large-caliber gun in a rotating turret. These requirements eventually produced the highly versatile tank designated Panzer IV.

PANZER IV

German industry built almost 9,000 Panzer IVs between 1936 and early 1945. During that time the Panzer IV served as the backbone of the German tank forces. The Panzer IV was designed from the start to allow for continual upgrades during production.

This farsighted design concept acknowledged that the German army knew it could not accurately predict its future needs. In contrast, the failure of the Allies to provide for growth in their tank designs resulted in the wholesale

The British Army Museum houses this Panzer III Ausf. L armed with a 50-mm gun. The vehicle is shown in a paint scheme similar to the early German army panzer gray. Along with the more powerful gun, the Ausf. L version of the Panzer III featured increased armor protection both on the superstructure front as well as turret mantlet. *British Army Tank Museum*

obsolescence of many Allied tanks in the early part of World War II.

The long-term success of one tank design over another can generally be ascribed to the balance between three important military characteristics: firepower, mobility, and protection. These factors are always in conflict with one another. Added to the mix are constraints of overall size and weight imposed by the necessity for road, rail, and water transport. Dozens of other constraints result in a final design that is always a compromise.

Fortunately for the German military and tank-producing industry, the design of the Panzer IV was heavily influenced by the ideas of General Heinz Guderian. Considered the father of the German military's tank forces, Guderian established the order of priorities for all German tank designs as: 1) mobility, 2) firepower, 3) armor protection, and 4) communications (radios). These priorities were successfully translated into the final design of the Panzer IV.

The suspension system on the Panzer IV consisted of 16 bogie wheels, eight on either side of the hull. The bogie wheels were paired together in suspension assemblies, four on either side of the hull. The suspension assemblies were attached to longitudinal twin quarter-elliptic leaf

A Panzer IV Ausf. F1 as it appeared in North Africa. A lighter sand color has been sprayed on irregularly over the original panzer gray. The vehicle is armed with a 75-mm howitzer. Compared to earlier versions of the Panzer IV series of medium tanks, the Ausf. F featured an increase in armor protection. To compensate for the additional weight of the steel armor, the vehicle had slightly wider tracks. *George Bradford*

An up-gunned Panzer IV Ausf. D armed with a long-barreled 75-mm gun. The vehicle forms part of the British Army Tank Museum's impressive collection. The original armament of the Ausf. D version of the Panzer IV consisted of a short-barreled 75-mm howitzer. Notice the drum-shaped commander's cupola with eight vision slits, at the rear of the vehicle's turret. *British Army Tank Museum*

springs bolted to the vehicle's hull. Above the bogie wheels were eight track return rollers, four on either side of the hull.

Guderian was also convinced that the best-designed tank in the world is not a truly effective weapon system unless a highly trained and motivated crew operates it. To this end, Guderian insisted that only the most promising men be recruited into the Panzertruppen (tank forces). This elite tank force was unmatched during most of World War II. It was the high quality of German tank crews that often gave them a winning advantage even when seriously outnumbered and outgunned.

Compared with other tanks of the day, the Panzer IV had a large turret. This design feature allowed for a five-man crew, three of which were in the turret. The turret crew consisted of the vehicle commander, a gunner, and a loader. The addition of a gunner in the turret allowed the vehicle commander to concentrate on the battlefield situation rather than on firing the gun. The British army first pioneered the three-man turret crew. Other armies stuck with the far less satisfactory practice of having only one or two men in a tank turret. Eventually, the superiority of the three-man turret crew became evident and was adopted by other tank-producing countries during World War II.

Seen here at Aberdeen Proving Ground, Maryland, shortly after World War II is this Panzer IV Ausf. G still in its original wartime colors. Around the vehicle's turret, which is facing rearward in this picture, are thin steel armor plates designed to act as stand-off protection from Soviet antitank rifles. The long, horizontal metal bar visible just below the turret was used to support similar standoff armor plates designed to protect the hull and suspension system. *Charles Kliment collection*

A Panzer IV Ausf. G in a storage yard at the French Army Tank Museum. It retains the thin steel armor plates known to the Germans as Schuerzen around its turret. The turret of the Panzer IV had a floor that was attached by brackets to the turret ring and thus rotated with the turret as it turned. Underneath the turret floor of the Panzer IV were the vehicle's three fuel tanks. *Ground Power Magazine*

The driver and the radio operator of the Panzer IV were located in the front of the hull. The radio operator also manned the 7.92-mm machine gun. Crew communication within the vehicle was through an intercom system consisting of earphones and throat microphones. This same system was employed in other German tanks during World War II. The five-man crew division of labor within the Panzer IV would be copied in all subsequent German World War II tanks.

When first conceived, the German army saw the Panzer IV medium tank as a support vehicle for the more numerous Panzer II light tanks. The vehicle was originally designed to carry a low-velocity short-barreled 75-mm howitzer. It could fire a high-explosive round out to a fair range. However, this weapon was not effective against tank armor.

The Germans originally designed the Panzer IV to deal with enemy machine gun and antitank gun positions. In contrast, the 20-mm gun on

This beautifully restored and operational Panzer IV Ausf. G belongs to the German Army Tank Museum. The vehicle was captured by the British army in North Africa in 1942 and returned to the German army in 1960 as a gesture of good will between the two former enemies. The vehicle was repainted in a color scheme similar to what it would have had during its wartime service. Clearly visible in the pictures are the vehicle's eight paired bogie wheels, as well as the front drive sprocket and rear idler wheel. *Thomas Anderson*

A beautifully restored Hummel (Bumblebee) belonging to the German Army Tank Museum. The vehicle was captured by the American army in Europe during World War II and shipped to Fort Knox, Kentucky, the long-time home of the U.S. Army Armor School. After the war, the vehicle formed part of the famous Patton Museum of Cavalry and Armor. In a gesture of good will between armies, the vehicle was loaned to the German Army Tank Museum in 1976. *Thomas Anderson*

the Panzer II fired only a non-explosive round. This meant its usefulness was limited, since it required a direct hit to do any damage at all. High-explosive rounds were able to damage anything within their blast effect range.

Panzer IVs fitted with a 75-mm howitzer were designated Ausf. A through F-1. These variants saw service in all German theaters of operation between 1939 and 1942. It was not until the German invasion of the Soviet Union in June 1941 that the Germans realized how poorly armed the early versions of the Panzer IV were against the more modern Soviet medium and

heavy tanks. In response to more potent threats, the Germans modified the Panzer IV turrets to accept a 75-mm gun, capable of firing both high-explosive and armor-piercing rounds. Extra armor was also added to the hull and turret for protection from more powerful enemy tank and antitank guns. The added weight required wider tracks to keep ground pressure within reasonable limits. With this upgrade, the Panzer IV Ausf. F-2 entered production in March 1942. Two hundred Ausf. F-2s rolled out of German factories before the next version entered production.

On display at the entrance of the French Army Museum is this Panzer IV Ausf. H. A visible outward distinction between the Ausf. H and the earlier Ausf. G was the elimination of some vision blocks in the vehicle's turret and superstructure. These features were made redundant by the normal addition of thin armored skirts to the vehicle's hull and turret. The Ausf. H version of the Panzer IV also featured a different type of rear idler wheel and all steel return rollers. *Ground Power Magazine*

Today, sophisticated target acquisition systems instantly calculate target distance and other important variables. During World War II, tank commanders and gunners had to quickly estimate the range to a target and the effects of wind, relative elevation, and other variables on the trajectory of a projectile. For longer-range targets, this imprecise technique usually resulted in the gunner firing a few trial rounds before hitting the target.

German tank crews enjoyed a marked advantage in the process of acquiring targets due to the superiority of their optics devices. This superiority allowed them to identify and open fire on opposing tanks long before an enemy tanker could respond. A World War II U.S. Army sergeant reported his impression of German tank-mounted optic devices: "The German telescopic sight mounted in their tanks is superior to ours. In particular it is more powerful—in fact all of their optical equipment is superior to ours."

Most versions of the Panzer IV used an electric motor to traverse the heavy three-man turret. The electric motor received its power from a small two-cycle gasoline engine generator located within the hull of the vehicle. A

This rare old picture shows a Hummel (Bumblebee) in its original wartime colors at Aberdeen Proving Ground shortly after World War II. To make room at the rear of the lengthened Panzer IV chassis for the gun crew, the engine was moved to the center of the vehicle's hull. The long-barreled 150-mm howitzer was mounted in the center of the vehicle over the engine compartment. *Charles Kliment collection*

Currently on display at the U.S. Army Ordnance Museum is this Brummbar (Grizzly Bear) armed with a 150-mm howitzer. The vehicle was brought to Aberdeen Proving Ground for test and evaluation purposes during World War II. After the war it was set aside with other vehicles for historical display purposes. It now forms part of the collection of the U.S. Army Ordnance Museum. There are long-term plans to repaint all the vehicles at the Ordnance Museum in more historically accurate colors when funding becomes available. *Michael Green*

A Hornisse (Hornet) tank destroyer currently on display at the U.S. Army Ordnance Museum. Visible is the tall and bulky superstructure of the vehicle that partially enclosed the 88-mm gun and its crew. This open-topped vehicle has suffered gravely from the ravages of time and weather while on outside display at the museum. *Michael Green*

hand-operated traverse system provided emergency backup in case the motor or generator failed. This same turret traverse system was employed on other German tanks such as the Panther medium tank.

Panzer IV Ausf. G, H, and J versions followed the Ausf. F-2. German industry built 1,687 of the Ausf. G version between May 1942 and June 1943. The Ausf. H, featuring a more powerful high-velocity long-barreled 75-mm gun, was the most common version of the Panzer IV with 3,774 produced between April 1943 and July 1944. The Ausf. J was the final production version of the Panzer IV. It was produced between June 1944 and March 1945 with a production run of 1,758 vehicles.

The Panzer IV Ausf. J weighed over 26 tons. This was a gain of almost 9 tons from the original Panzer IV. Most of the weight gain came from additional armor. To this day, the balance between armor weight and vehicle mobility is a continual compromise with all tank designs.

SELECTED PANZER IV VARIANTS

Modified Panzer IV chassis were employed by the German army for a wide range of special purposes including command vehicles, antiaircraft platforms, and ammunition carriers. The best-known Panzer IV–based weapon systems were self-propelled howitzers and tank destroyers.

This rare picture shot at Aberdeen Proving Ground shortly after World War II shows an early production example of a Panzer IV/70(V) tank destroyer in its original wartime colors. The visual clue that marks this as an early production model is the four track return rollers. Later production models featured only three track return rollers. The long barrel on this vehicle has been broken off. This vehicle was cut up by the U.S. Army during a Korean War scrap drive. *Charles Kliment collection*

On display at a British military vehicle show in 1998 is this nicely restored Panzer IV/70(V). Until recently the vehicle belonged to the British army's School of Tank Technology; it was traded to the Patton Museum of Cavalry and Armor. The vehicle has only three track return rollers, indicating that it is a later production vehicle. The camouflage scheme on the vehicle is based on the colors it had when captured by the British army during World War II. *Panzer Prints*

The slightly lengthened chassis of the Panzer IV was a nearly ideal carrier for heavy artillery pieces such as howitzers. One of the two major German artillery systems, the Hummel (Bumblebee), entered service in 1941. The Hummel fit into the German Panzerartillerie category.

Hummel armament was a limited-traverse 150-mm howitzer that fired a 95.9-pound high-explosive round to a maximum range of 14,572 yards. The five-man gun crew was protected by thin armor plates on the front and sides. Due to space constraints, the vehicle could only carry 18 rounds of howitzer ammunition. Additional ammunition was brought forward by a resupply version of the Hummel.

The other major Panzer IV–based artillery system was the Sturmpanzer IV, also known as the Brummbar (Grizzly Bear). It was armed with a limited-traverse 150-mm howitzer enclosed in a fully armored box-like superstructure. Unlike the indirect-fire Hummel, the short-range howitzer on the Brummbar was used as a close-

range direct-fire weapon to support infantry units. German industry would build 306 of the vehicles between April 1943 and March 1945.

Besides using the Panzer IV as a chassis for self-propelled artillery, the German army also used it as the basic for a Panzerjaeger called the Hornisse (Hornet) that carried their famous 88-mm gun in a limited-traverse mount. The Hornisse was fielded in late 1943. On Hitler's personal order, the Hornisse was renamed the Nashorn (Rhinoceros) to suit its more aggressive role on the battlefield. German industry built 494 Hornisse/Nashorn vehicles between February 1943 and March 1945.

Like other early-model German Panzerjaegers, the Hornisse/Nashorn was rushed into service with thin armor plates on the front and sides of the 88-mm gun. The vehicle's large size and height, combined with inadequate armor protection, made it an easy target for almost any enemy weapon.

Among the vehicle's weak points, stated by a British army report issued in October 1944, were

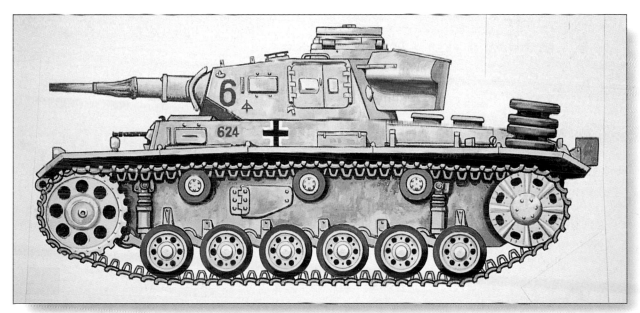

A Panzer III Ausf. F as it would have appeared during the fighting in North Africa between the British and German armies in 1941 and 1942. The Ausf. F version of the Panzer III first appeared in service in 1939 armed with a 37-mm antitank gun. These were later replaced on many vehicles with a low-velocity short-barreled 50-mm antitank gun like the one shown in this drawing. *George Bradford*

This late production Panzer IV/70(V) can be seen in its original camouflage colors in another rare old picture taken at Aberdeen Proving Ground after World War II. This vehicle survives to this day and is currently on outside display at the U.S. Army Ordnance Museum. The paint scheme in which it arrived has long since been painted over with little regard for historical accuracy. *Charles Kliment collection*

frequent breakdowns because the vehicle's chassis was both underpowered and unreliable, with a limited endurance of only 950 miles before a major overhaul was needed. The fact that the gun crew on the vehicle, except for the loader, were all highly trained specialists with extensive training meant any casualties could severely degrade the weapon's effectiveness.

On the positive side, the strong points of the Nashorn, stated by the report, included its very effective gun and ammunition. Every hit with the vehicle's 88-mm gun on an enemy tank meant a penetration. The high-explosive (HE) round fired from the gun had a very good fragmentation effect. In a pinch, the gun could also be used as an artillery piece up to an effective range of 11,000 yards.

In late 1943, the German army fielded the 24-ton purpose-built Jagdpanzer IV armed with a limited-traverse 75-mm gun. It was crewed by four men and consisted of a low-slung armored superstructure fitted to the top of a Panzer IV chassis.

The height of the vehicle was only 6 feet 5.2 inches. Its low silhouette and well-sloped armor made it a tough target for Allied tankers. An example of how hard it was to kill a Jagdpanzer IV was given by an American lieutenant in a late-war interview. His platoon of five M-4 Sherman tanks fired 27 rounds of armor-piercing ammunition at a Jagdpanzer IV and failed to penetrate its frontal armor. German industry would build 1,725 Jagdpanzer IVs between January 1944 and March 1945.

PANZER III

After laying the groundwork for the design of the Panzer IV medium tank in 1934, German tank designers discovered that French heavy tank armor was able to defeat both the 20-mm gun in the Panzer II light tank and the 75-mm howitzer mounted in the Panzer IV medium support tank. In response, the German army introduced the Panzer III medium tank in 1935. It resembled a slightly scaled-down version of the Panzer IV, with the same crew layout of five men.

The Panzer III was 17 feet 8 inches long, 9 feet 9 inches wide, and 8 feet 3 inches high. The suspension system on all but the earliest versions consisted of 12 small, road wheels, six on either side of the hull. The road wheels were sprung by torsion bars. There were also three small return rollers on either side of the hull.

A Maybach 12-cylinder engine produced about 300 horsepower, which gave most versions of the Panzer III a top road speed of about 25 miles per hour. Early versions of the Panzer III weighed in at roughly 13 tons. Later versions were fitted with additional armor protection that nearly doubled the weight. Primarily because the chassis could not handle the extra weight, the Panzer III was a design dead end and remained in production for only 6 years. Although it was not as successful in service as

This wonderfully restored Panzer III Ausf. M belongs to the German Army Tank Museum. It features a sand color common to German tanks seeing service in North Africa. The vehicle was acquired from Libya in 1986. This version of the Panzer III can be distinguished from the very similar Ausf. L by the three-rack smoke dischargers mounted on the sides of the turret. The Ausf. L had its five-rack smoke dischargers fitted to the rear of its hull. *Thomas Anderson*

the more numerous Mark IVs, the Panzer III tank proved very effective against the poorly designed British army early-war tanks during the fighting in North Africa between 1941 and 1942.

Panzer III Ausf. A, B, C, and D were trial versions for purposes of refining the final production configuration. Panzer III Ausf. E was the first version produced in volume. Ausf. F through Ausf. N upgrades quickly followed. The most common Panzer III version was the Ausf. J with 1,549 units built between March 1941 and July 1942.

The most prominent difference between the various versions of the Panzer III was the main armament. Ausf. A through Ausf. G were armed with a 37-mm gun. This was a version of the German army's standard pre–World War II towed antitank gun. Combat experience would soon show that this weapon was unable to penetrate the armor of enemy tanks.

Starting with the Ausf. H version in October 1940, Panzer IIIs incorporated a 50-mm gun. This gun also proved ineffective as a tank killer and was replaced in the middle of Ausf. J production with a longer, improved 50-mm gun. This armament configuration continued through Ausf. M production. Many earlier Panzer IIIs were retrofitted with the longer 50-mm antitank gun to improve their battlefield effectiveness.

A secret Allied report dated October 1944 described the Panzer III Ausf. G and its turret arrangement:

The fighting compartment surmounted by the turret is in the centre. On the Pz.Kpfw. III there is no floor in the turret, although seats for the commander and gunner are suspended from the turret wall. The loader, who stands on the right-hand side of the gun, has no seat and must therefore walk around with the turret as it traverses. The gunner sits forward on the left-hand side of

A Panzer III Ausf. N in a pea green color common to German tanks in the last stages of the fighting in North Africa in 1943. The biggest difference between the Ausf. N version of the Panzer III and earlier versions was the mounting of a 75-mm howitzer in its turret. Due to the weight of the howitzer, the Germans dispensed with the extra armor on the vehicle's mantlet. *George Bradford*

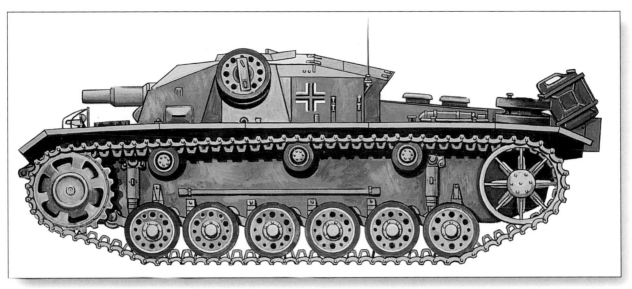

Shown in this color artwork is a very early StuG. III Ausf. D that saw service in North Africa in 1943 before its capture by the British army. It was armed with a 75-mm howitzer that reflected its original design role as an infantry support weapon. The vehicle had a crew of four men and carried 44 rounds of main gun ammunition onboard. *George Bradford*

the gun. The 5 cm gun is fired electrically by means of a trigger on the turret traverse hand wheel, and the coaxial MG mechanically by a foot-operated trigger. The commander sits in the middle at the rear of the turret. His cupola is integral with the turret, and six ports fitted with bulletproof glass blocks and sliding steel shutters provide all-round vision. The cupola hatch consists of two hinged flaps. An auxiliary turret-traversing handle on the loader's side allows dual control for quick traversing, as no power traverse is provided on this tank.

By early 1942 it was very clear to the German army that even the improved longer 50-mm gun fitted to the J through M versions of the Panzer III was ineffective against the Soviet army's medium and heavy tanks. In response, the Germans mounted a 75-mm howitzer in the Panzer III. With this change in armament the vehicle was designated the Panzer III Ausf. N. German industry would build 663 examples of the Panzer III Ausf. N between June 1942 and August 1943.

Thirty-seven additional vehicles were also constructed from earlier rebuilt versions of the Panzer III.

The 75 mm howitzer on the Ausf. N fired a far more potent high-explosive round than the 50-mm gun on earlier versions of the Panzer III. It could also fire a wartime-developed shaped-charge antitank round.

Selected Panzer III Variants

The Panzer III chassis was employed in a number of different roles including command center, flame-thrower, ammunition supply, and antiaircraft. The best-known and most widely deployed variant of the Panzer III chassis was a turretless assault gun: the Sturmgeschuetz or StuG. III.

The StuG. III assault gun requirements were established in 1936. Five prototypes, designated Ausf. A, appeared the next year. The first early-production vehicles rolled out of the factory between January 1940 and May 1940. Volume production began with the Ausf. B version in June

This slightly overhead picture of a StuG. III Ausf. G illustrates many rear hull details not seen in wartime pictures of the vehicle. Visible is the one-piece hatch on the vehicle commander's cupola. Earlier versions of the StuG. III series did not have a commander's cupola, which needlessly forced the vehicle commander to expose his head to enemy fire when he wished to check outside his vehicle. *Panzer Prints*

1940. By May 1945, German industry had built more than 9,000 StuG. IIIs in various versions.

Early versions of the StuG. III (Ausf. A through E) were armed with a 75-mm howitzer. This gun reflected the original role of the StuG. III as an offensive infantry support weapon, and it was successfully employed during the invasion of France in May 1940.

In a report completed during World War II, the U.S. Army described how the Germans regarded the StuG. III in the infantry support role, as

a decisive weapon to be employed at the forefront of an attack. Working together with the infantry, the StuG. III was designed to break through enemy defensive lines. Its biggest advantage was its ability to follow the infantry right up to the objective. Once in sight of the objective, the crew of the StuG. III was to use its gun at short range to destroy enemy weapon emplacements that hindered the infantry's advance. The Germans normally preferred to use their assault guns in large numbers for mutual support rather than singly.

This beautifully preserved example of a StuG. III Ausf. G belongs to the collection of the Military Vehicle Technology Center in Northern California. The vehicle was completely rebuilt from the ground up by a team of highly skilled mechanics. No effort was spared while attempting to restore the vehicle to its original wartime appearance. *Michael Green*

Since the assault gun concept originated with the artillery branch of the German army before World War II, the StuG. III was manned by a specially trained artillery crew rather than panzer troops. Experience gained during the fighting in France clearly demonstrated to the German army that its tank and antitank weapons did not possess the hitting power or range necessary to kill enemy tanks from anywhere but close range. Early engagements with well-armored Russian tanks during the invasion of the Soviet Union in the summer of 1941 only reconfirmed this fact. This would result in a widespread demand for upgrades to the armament on most of Germany's armored fighting vehicles. Krupp developed a more powerful 75-mm gun that was compatible with the StuG. III chassis. In late 1941, the new gun was mounted on the Ausf. F version of the StuG. III. Between March and September of 1942, 359 units were built.

On display at the Wehrtechnische Studiensammlung (WTS) in Koblenz, Germany, is this fully restored late production model StuG. III Ausf. G. The vehicle is fitted with the thin steel-armored skirts typically found on these vehicles during World War II and the antimagnetic paste called Zimmerit. The biggest visual clue to identifying late production examples of the StuG. III Ausf. G is the cast armored mantlet, nicknamed the Saukopf (pig's head) by German soldiers. *Panzer Prints*

This vehicle was a highly effective tank destroyer. Between March 1942 and the end of the war in Europe, StuG. III vehicles armed with new 75-mm guns accounted for more enemy tank kills than all the other different-turreted German tanks combined.

The Ausf. F version of the StuG. III was followed by a version with extra armor called the Ausf. F/8. Production totaled 334 vehicles and ran between September and December of 1942.

Despite their success as tank destroyers, the StuG. III Ausf. F and F/8 were never officially classified by the German army as Panzerjaegers or as Jadgpanzers. This situation reflected the fact that many German self-propelled weapon systems like the StuG. III series were forced by military necessity to serve dual purposes. On some occasions the Germans made up for shortages of tanks in their panzer divisions with StuG. III vehicles.

The most common version of the StuG. III was the final production model designated Ausf. G, with 7,720 produced before Germany's surrender in May of 1945. The StuG. III Ausf. G was 17 feet 9 1/2 inches long (excluding the gun), 9 feet 8 inches wide, and 7 feet tall. It had a crew of four and weighed about 26 tons. The frontal armor of the vehicle's low-slung superstructure was a little over 3 inches thick. The armament of the StuG. III Ausf. G consisted of a 75-mm gun. Protection from infantry on the StuG. III Ausf. G came from a roof-mounted 7.92-mm machine gun, later changed to a coaxial 7.92-mm machine gun.

Some StuG. III Ausf. F and G chassis were fitted with limited-traverse 105-mm howitzers. This configuration was designated as the 10.5 Sturmhaubitze (assault howitzer) 42. Between October 1942 and February 1945, 1,211 assault howitzers were built.

PANZER V PANTHER

The biggest surprise for the U.S. Army after the June 6, 1944, invasion of France (D-Day) was encountering the German Panzer V medium tank. American tank crews who faced it in battle feared the Panzer V as a formidable and deadly adversary. Sergeant Rains M. Robbins, an American M-4 Sherman medium tank commander, and his driver Corporal Walter McGrail described their first impressions of the Panzer V in a wartime report:

The German Mark V tank, mounting a 75-mm gun with a muzzle velocity of about 3200 feet per second, is able to travel on a highway at 38 mph, 15 to 20-mph cross-country in soft going, and better as the going improves.

It has to our mind greater maneuverability, being able to turn in the space it's sitting in, while our mediums require half a field. It also has more armor protection, with approximately four inches of armor on its front end and enough rearward slope to make it the equivalent of six to seven inches. The consensus of opinion is that the German Mark V can outspeed, outmaneuver and outgun us, in addition to their added protection of heavier armor.

In early 1944 a personal directive from Hitler ordered the Panzer V designation be dropped, and the vehicle thereafter be designated only as the "Panther" tank. The German policy of applying "cat" names (such as Tiger, Lynx, and Leopard) to tanks and tank destroyers began in 1942 as a propaganda tool to catch the public's fancy. Insect names (such as Cricket, Hornet, and Bumblebee) were reserved for self-propelled artillery pieces.

To determine what it would take to destroy a Panther, General Omar Bradley's First Army took captured vehicles to test sites and fired every weapon in their inventory at them. To their dismay, only the most potent projectiles fired at close range would penetrate the thick, well-sloped frontal armor of the vehicle.

Beginning in early March 1943, German industry began production of a StuG. III Ausf. G fitted with a 105-mm howitzer in place of the standard 75-mm gun. In this new configuration, the vehicle was designated a Sturmhaubitze (assault howitzer). This example was shown on outside display at the Patton Museum of Cavalry and Armor sometime in the early 1970s. The vehicle was placed into interior storage sometime in the 1980s. *Dean and Nancy Kleffman*

The only American weapons that could kill a Panther from the front at a realistic range were the army's towed 90-mm antiaircraft gun and the 105-mm howitzer firing a shaped-charge warhead. However, the army could not spare 105-mm howitzers from their artillery fire support duties. This left only the 90-mm antiaircraft gun. Unfortunately, this weapon was large and cumbersome and was difficult to set up and fire. Despite this problem, Bradley positioned a number of 90-mm gun units behind his First Army's front lines to defend from any

Pictured on display at the Swiss Army Tank Museum is this early production example of the Panther Ausf. A. The driver had a direct vision armored flap in the front hull plate of the vehicle, which measured about 10x4 inches. When enemy fire forced the closure of this flap, he could use two periscopes in the hull roof above his head. The radio operator, who sat next to the driver, could fire an onboard 7.92-mm machine gun through a much smaller vertical armored flap. *Andreas Kirchhoff*

breakthroughs by German Panther or Tiger tanks in July 1944.

It was not until September 1944 that the U.S. Army fielded a tank destroyer that could take out a Panther tank at other than close range. This vehicle was the full-tracked M-36 armed with a turret-mounted version of the army's 90-mm antiaircraft gun. Until the M-36 entered service, it fell upon the crews of older generations of American tank destroyers to fight it out with German Panther tanks. A U.S. Army report issued prior to September 1944 stated: "To destroy a Panther, a tank destroyer with a three inch [M-10] or 76-mm gun [M-18] would have to aim for the side or rear of the turret, the opening through which the hull-mounted machine gun projected, or for the underside of the gun shield [mantlet]."

One has to wonder how the Panther, which was first produced in late 1942, could prove so superior to American tanks and most tank destroyers as late as 1945. Part of the answer lies in the fact that the Panther design was based on German experience fighting on the eastern front, where large and frequent tank battles had been raging for years. The gun-armor race between German and Soviet tank designers had been conducted at a feverish pace since early 1942. It resulted in the progressive advent of tanks with thicker armor and ever larger and more powerful guns.

On display at the French Army Tank Museum is this late production Panther Ausf. A. The clean sloping lines of the Panther tank have made it a long-time favorite among legions of tank modelers and buffs. The Ausf. A version of the Panther first appeared in August 1943. Production models were built by four different companies including MAN, Daimler-Benz, MNH, and DEMAG. *Ground Power Magazine*

Taking part in an open-house display at the German Army Tank Museum is this operational Panther Ausf. A. The extra radio antennas at the rear of the hull are evidence that this tank is configured as a command vehicle. The vehicle was acquired from the Swedish Army Museum in 1961. Clearly seen in this picture is the long (19 feet 2 1/4 inch) barrel of the vehicle's powerful 75-mm gun. *Thomas Anderson*

The impetus for the creation of the well-known Panther medium tank was the German army's complete surprise on meeting the Soviet army's revolutionary T-34 medium tank in the summer of 1941. This vehicle managed to make the entire existing German inventory of tanks obsolete almost overnight. Pictured on display at the U.S. Army Ordnance Museum is the original version of the T-34 armed with a 76.2-mm gun. *Michael Green*

It was the introduction of the Soviet army's well-designed and extremely capable T-34 medium tank (originally armed with a 76-mm main gun and later upgraded to an 85-mm main gun) that inspired the design of the German Panther tank.

Many historians, as well as postwar tank designers and engineers, describe the T-34 tank as embodying the perfect balance of firepower, mobility, and protection. Despite its many excellent features, the T-34 tank had shortcomings that the Germans were able to exploit in battle. However, the T-34 was far superior to the German Panzer III and IV medium tanks that were the mainstay of the panzer divisions in 1941 and 1942.

In contrast to the armored box-like construction of the German tanks designed before 1941, the T-34 had a well-sloped armor arrangement that greatly heightened its resistance to German antitank rounds. This feature would be copied in the design of the Panther tank as well as other German tanks and tank destroyers after 1942.

The Panther in many ways followed the conventional design features, such as crew layout and gasoline engine, of earlier German tanks. The Panther designers, however, became more daring and copied the unique design features of the T-34, including its well-sloped armor arrangement and the large individually-sprung road wheels with high wheel travel (which improved the vehicle's cross-country speed). The Panther tank suspension system consisted of eight double-interleaved road wheels on each

Visible in this rare old picture is a Jagdpanther at Aberdeen Proving Ground, in its original colors, sometime shortly after World War II. The vehicle is currently on display at the U.S. Army Ordnance Museum. Over the years, the vehicle has been repainted numerous times with little regard for historical accuracy. Like other military vehicles that have been on outside display at the museum, it steadily deteriorated over the years. *Charles Kliment collection*

side of the hull connected by twin independent torsion bars. As with all other German tanks it had front sprockets and rear idlers.

The Soviet army supplied the British and American armies with information on the Panther as early as July 1943. This was shortly after the German military deployed the first production batch of Panthers during the well-known Kursk offensive in July 1943, which resulted in the biggest tank battles of World War II.

A British wartime report dated October 10, 1943, based on Soviet army intelligence, describes the hull design of the Panther tank: "Russian influence is very noticeable in the design of the hull which resembles that of the Russian T-34. In both the T-34 and Panther, the plates are similarly sloped so as to present the most difficult angle of attack."

Like other German tanks, the Panther would be progressively improved during its production

WEAPON DEFINITIONS

A howitzer is normally a comparatively short cannon with a medium muzzle velocity and a curved trajectory. The higher angle of fire, often referred to as indirect fire, allows the weapon to reach targets hidden from flat trajectory (direct fire) guns. Howitzers are generally employed to fire high-explosive (HE) projectiles and not armor-piercing (AP) projectiles.

For antitank purposes, howitzers can fire a shaped-charge projectile, consisting of an explosive charge with a lined hollow cone at the nose end, which develops a high-velocity jet upon detonation. Unlike an armor-piercing projectile that punches a hole through armor plate, a shaped-charge projectile instead burns a hole through armor plate.

A mortar is a cannon with a short barrel, usually smooth bore, and a low muzzle velocity. It is fired at high elevation and has a higher angle of fire and shorter range than a howitzer. It is used to reach nearby targets that are protected or concealed by intervening hills or other short-range barriers.

The term *gun* generally applies to all firearms, but in its more restricted and technical sense, it refers to a cannon with a relatively long barrel, fired from a carriage or mount. Compared to a howitzer, a gun normally has a longer barrel, a flat trajectory, and a more limited maximum elevation (except antiaircraft guns). It is used either for long-range fire, or in the case of tanks, for the delivery of fire requiring a flat trajectory and high velocity. Tank guns can fire both armor-piercing and high-explosive projectiles. Most armor-piercing projectiles contain high-explosive elements within them.

Not all tank guns are created equally. Merely because a tank gun has a bore diameter of 75 millimeters (2.92 inches) does not mean it will have the same performance characteristics as other 75-mm guns. The performance parameter of a 75-mm gun on a late-war German tank was far superior to a similar-caliber weapon mounted on an earlier-war tank. More important when determining the effectiveness of a tank gun are its design, the materials used in building it, how it was built, the type of ammunition used, how long the barrel is, and what type of fire control system is used to aim and fire it at targets.

Within the German army during World War II there was a constant effort to improve the performance of tank guns, resulting in numerous variations of a basic design. For example, there were at least several progressively improved versions of the famous 88-mm gun in service with the German army during World War II.

In general, the best way to improve the performance of a particular tank gun is to increase its muzzle velocity (how fast a projectile leaves the barrel of a tank gun). The higher the muzzle velocity, the faster and harder the projectile will strike its intended target.

Muzzle velocity can be improved in different ways, such as lightening a projectile or adding a more powerful propellant (powder). A very common World War II method of improving muzzle velocity was to lengthen the barrel of a tank gun. For example, the 75-mm gun on the famous German Panther tank was 19 feet 2 1/4 inches long and could fire an armor-piercing projectile at a muzzle velocity of 3,675 feet per second. In comparison, the 75-mm gun mounted on the American M-4 Sherman tank was just over 7 feet long and fired an armor-piercing projectile at less than 2,030 feet per second.

Seen here on display at the British Army Tank Museum is a Jagdpanther (tank destroyer). The vehicle was realistically painted in a re-creation of a German wartime camouflage scheme. This vehicle was assembled after the war with Germany was over by local workers under British army supervision for test and evaluation purposes. *British Army Tank Museum*

run. As new versions came off the assembly line, they would be given different designations consistent with standard German military practice. The first preproduction prototype Panther tank, built by MAN, started tests in November of 1942.

The importance of rapidly fielding a large quantity of Panther tanks was so great, that Daimler-Benz, Henschel, and other German companies soon started producing Panthers. The three basic production versions of the Panther were labeled (for some reason out of sequence) Ausf. D, A, and G. By the end of the war in Europe, German industry managed to build an astounding 5,508 Panther tanks. The most common model was the Ausf. G, of which 3,740 were fielded before the war ended.

SELECTED PANTHER VARIANTS

As with other German tanks, the chassis of the Panther supported a variety of different missions. Variants using the Panther chassis included an armored recovery vehicle and a command vehicle.

The armored recovery version of the Panther, known as the Bergepanther, had no turret. Rather, the fighting compartment of the vehicle was enclosed by an open-topped box-like structure 32 inches high, 8 feet 1 inch wide, and 7 feet 6 inches long. The only armament on the Bergepanther were two 7.92-mm machine guns. By the time the war ended, German industry had built 347 examples of the armored recovery version of the Panther.

The command vehicle variant based on a modified Panther tank retained both its turret and main gun. To make room for the additional radios and associated generator in the vehicle, the number of main gun rounds was reduced to 64. German industry would build a total of 329 Panther tank command vehicles between late 1944 and early 1945.

Starting in February 1944 the Germans began production of a new Jagdpanzer known as the Jagdpanther (Hunting Panther) based on the Ausf. G version of the Panther chassis. The vehicle was armed with a limited-traverse 88-mm gun and a single hull-mounted 7.92-mm machine gun. German industry built 392 of these vehicles between January 1944 and March 1945.

A British army report dated September 6, 1944, describes the Jagdpanther:

One of the latest German SP [self-propelled] equipments to appear in action on any front, is an 8.8 cm Pak [antitank] 43 gun on a Panther chassis. The equipment consists of a recent type of normal Panther chassis, with a superimposed superstructure consisting virtually of a Panther glacis [front hull] plate and

This picture, shot in 1976, shows the one-of-a-kind Panther II tank belonging to the collection of the Patton Museum of Cavalry and Armor. The vehicle was restored to running condition by museum staff and volunteers in the early 1970s. For many years it was run once a year at the museum's annual living history show held every Fourth of July. Because of its rarity, the vehicle was eventually placed inside the museum for display purposes only. *Dean and Nancy Kleffman*

This nicely restored Jagdpanther belongs to the German Army Tank Museum. The gouges on its lower frontal armor show where it was hit by unknown antitank rounds that failed to penetrate. At the bottom of the mantlet is a hole showing that at least one round did penetrate the crew compartment. The well-sloped frontal hull armor plate on the Jagdpanther is 80 millimeters thick, and the gun mantlet is 100 millimeters thick. *Thomas Anderson*

superstructure sides continued upwards to form a spacious fighting compartment with a roof and sloping rear plate. A German document states that the equipment is designed for engaging important targets at long ranges from stationary positions, and that it should not be used in support of infantry or as an 'assault' gun. It adds that unarmored targets must invariably be engaged with HE [high explosive] ammunition, which constitutes half the total ammunition carried. A noticeable feature of the equipment is the amount of room available in the fighting compartment to enable the gun to be easily serviced, and the fact that all the elaborate observation facilities available are on the superstructure roof plate, there being no vision openings at the front or sides of the vehicle except for the driver's episcope [periscope] opening.

An unusual one-of-a-kind Panther tank variant generally called the Panther II is on display at the famous Patton Museum of Cavalry and Armor. It represents a 1943 German attempt to create a hybrid vehicle that would combine components from early Panther tanks with yet-to-be-built Tiger II heavy tanks.

Armor design improvements to later production models of the Panther tank, and delays in the production of the Tiger II heavy tank killed the project. Only one experimental prototype of the Panther II was built before Germany surrendered. It was discovered by American troops at the end of World War II and shipped to Aberdeen Proving Ground, Maryland, for technical evaluation. Eventually the vehicle was traded to the Patton Museum where it now resides on display.

Three

HEAVY TANKS

✦ ✦ ✦

Before giving the go-ahead for production of the very small and simple Panzer I light tank in 1932, the German army issued tentative requirements for a large heavy tank. At the time, German industry was unable to even consider such a project, so the heavy tank concept was dropped. However, the need for a heavy tank never disappeared.

Between 1937 and early 1941, the German firm of Henschel, under sponsorship by the German army ordnance department, undertook a series of experimental projects that focused on a viable medium tank design. This work resulted in the building and testing of a number of prototype vehicles. While none of these prototypes were considered for production, the effort gave Henschel valuable engineering experience in the design considerations for heavy tanks.

Hitler's growing interest in armored warfare was a strong factor in encouraging German industry to work on heavy tank designs. By the time

A Tiger II tank resides near the small Belgian village of La Gleize. The vehicle was abandoned during the Battle of the Bulge in December 1944. After the war it was incorporated into a local museum. Clearly visible in this picture is the very long turret of the Tiger II. The better-designed and simpler-to-produce series turret had a front armor plate 180 millimeters thick, and retained the 80-millimeter thickness on the turret sides (as found on the 50 earlier Krupp-designed turrets). *Andreas Kirchhoff*

Germany invaded the Soviet Union in June 1941, Hitler had already begun to use his position as head of the armed forces to intensify the German army's interest in heavy tank development.

THE ELEFANT

One of the items that attracted Hitler's attention was a set of requirements for a new heavy tank designated the VK 4501 project, issued a few weeks before the attack on the Soviet Union. The requirements of the project called for a vehicle weighing roughly 45 tons and featuring as its main armament a modified version of the already-proven German 88-mm antiaircraft gun. One of the conditions imposed on the German firms interested in the project was the need to complete a prototype in time for Hitler's birthday on April 20, 1942. Hitler's interest in the

This rare old picture, taken shortly after World War II, shows a late-model production Elefant in its original wartime paint scheme. The vehicle has been an important part of the U.S. Army Ordnance Museum for many decades. Considering the 65-ton weight of the vehicle, the Germans decided to power the vehicle with two Maybach gasoline engines, each producing 320 horsepower. The top speed of the vehicle was 12.5 miles per hour. The maximum range of the Elefant with a full load of fuel was about 90 miles. *Charles Kliment*

Visible in this close-up picture of one of only two Elefants still in existence, is the vehicle's hull-mounted 7.92-mm machine gun position. Of the 90 Elefants constructed by the German firm of Nibelungenwerke between April and May 1943, only 48 were upgraded with the hull machine gun. Another feature found on the rebuilt Elefants was a commander cupola—a feature not found on the original production vehicles. This vehicle, like so many others at the U.S. Army Ordnance Museum, has suffered from years of neglect and is slowly rusting away. *Michael Green*

project peaked after the invasion of the Soviet Union showed that the Russian T-34 medium tank had rendered the entire inventory of German tanks obsolete.

The German firms of Henschel and Porsche were both vying for the contract to build the new heavy tank. Dr. Ferdinand Porsche was so convinced that he would win the contract because of his personal friendship with Hitler, that he went ahead and built 90 turrets and hulls for his own heavy tank design. Tests of the competing

prototype vehicles soon confirmed that the Henschel vehicle was the superior vehicle. Therefore, Henschel—not Porsche—won the contract to build the German army's new heavy tank.

Ninety of Porsche's remaining chassis were bought by the German army and were converted by the German firm of Alkett into a combination assault gun and tank destroyer between April and May of 1943. The conversions consisted of relocating the engine compartment to the center and building a large, block-like armored superstructure at the rear of the vehicle to house an 88-mm gun in a limited-traverse mount. The vehicle was originally named the Ferdinand in honor of its designer. This was later changed to Elefant (Elephant) as an indication of its large size and weight.

Seen in this rare wartime color picture is the business end of the well-known Tiger I tank with its deadly high-velocity antitank gun. The 88-mm gun on the Tiger I was only one version of a family of German antiaircraft, antitank, and tank guns of that caliber in millimeters. The Germans themselves did not use the term *88*, but referred to these weapons as the 8.8-cm guns of various types. *Charles Kliment collection*

The Elefant weighed 65 tons and had a crew of six men. It was 26 feet 10 inches long (excluding gun), 11 feet 3 inches wide, and 9 feet 10 inches tall. Frontal armor was 200 millimeters thick with 80-millimeter side protection. Early models lacked hull-mounted machine guns for close-in defense, causing them to become easy prey for Soviet infantry tank-hunting teams. Its weight and size made it difficult to maneuver. The Elefant was considered to be a failure in German army service.

TIGER I

Production of the Henschel vehicle began in mid-1942. The new heavy tank was originally designated the Panzer VI Tiger Ausf. H1 in March 1942. In March 1943 the German Army changed the designation from Tiger H1 to the much more familiar Tiger I. The Ausf. designation was also changed from the original Ausf. H1 to Ausf. E. By this time, combat-loaded gross vehicle weight had increased to 57 tons from the original 45-ton design weight. This added weight imposed severe mobility and reliability penalties. For example, long forced marches were forbidden since they placed undue strain on the engine, transmission, and suspension systems.

As soon as the first production run of Tiger I heavy tanks rolled off the Henschel factory floor, Hitler quickly ordered them into action against the Soviet army. Their debut on August 29, 1942, was a dismal failure because they were committed in a very small number (only four were available) to an area of marshy ground completely unsuitable to their heavy weight and large bulk. On this day's outing three of the Tigers broke down with mechanical problems. After all four vehicles were withdrawn from service and repaired, they were once again committed to action on September 22, 1942, in the same general area. On this second operation, all four Tigers were either knocked out by Soviet antitank guns or became bogged down in the soft ground. Three of the vehicles were recovered from the battlefields, while the fourth vehicle was destroyed in

A very popular exhibit at the British Army Tank Museum is this impressive-looking Tiger I tank. The British army in North Africa captured the vehicle in early 1943. It was the first vehicle of its kind acquired by the British and was returned to England for extensive testing and evaluation before being passed on to the museum's collection. Clearly visible are the vehicle's wide steel service tracks designed to support its 56 tons in the field. *British Army Tank Museum*

place by the Germans to prevent it from falling into Soviet hands.

Despite Hitler's initial disappointment with the German heavy tank's combat debut, which rested squarely on his own shoulders, the Tiger I was soon to prove its worth in battlefield tactical settings better suited to its design limitations. The optimum combat situation in which the Tiger I excelled was one where the crew could take advantage of its first-rate optical sights and long-range gun on hard, open terrain to destroy enemy tanks before they could return effective fire with their shorter-ranged weapons.

The U.S. Army would first meet the Tiger I with its deadly 88-mm gun in Tunisia (North Africa) in late 1943. Its effectiveness made a strong impression on almost every American tanker who had the misfortune of meeting it in battle. An American colonel stated, "I have inspected the battlefield at Faid Pass in Tunisia, being with the force which retook it. Inspection of our tanks destroyed there indicated

The Germans found it impossible to ship the Tiger I tank by rail because of the excessive width of its service tracks (12 feet 3 inches). This forced them to design a much narrower set of tracks for rail shipment purposes as seen here on a late-model production example of the vehicle on display at the French Army Tank Museum. When shipped by rail, the Germans also removed the tank's outer set of road wheels as well as its mudguards. *Ground Power Magazine*

Seen here on temporary display at the Wehrtechnische Studiensammlung (WTS) museum in Germany, in 1995, is a very early initial production example of a Tiger I. The vehicle was originally found abandoned by American troops in North Africa in March 1943. To perform an in-depth study of the vehicle, it was shipped back to the United States for test and evaluation purposes. The vehicle later became part of the U.S. Army Ordnance Museum at Aberdeen Proving Ground, Maryland. *Andreas Kirchhoff*

that the 88-mm gun penetrated into the turret from the front and out again in the rear. Few gouges were found indicating that all strikes had made penetrations."

Between July 1942 and August 1944, German industry built 1,354 Tiger I tanks. Most of these vehicles were immediately shipped to the eastern front. From the summer of 1941 until the closing stages of the war the bulk of the German army, including its panzer divisions, were committed to fighting the Soviet army.

In the field, Tiger I tanks were organized into heavy battalions of 59 tanks each. It was originally intended that each panzer division would be assigned a Tiger I battalion. Due to the high cost of the vehicle and its complexity, German industry was unable to produce the number of Tiger I tanks needed. Instead, only a handful of elite army or Waffen SS panzer divisions had a Tiger I tank battalion permanently assigned. Most Tiger I battalions were assigned to army group commands and attached to subordinate units such as corps and divisions for specific missions only. Once a mission was completed, the Tiger battalions reverted to army group command.

To make the Tiger I tanks easier for the manufacturers to build, the Germans designed the thick steel armored plates on the hull of the Tiger I to run vertically. Only after meeting the Soviet T-34 medium tank in battle did the German designers really realize the advantages of sloping the armor on their tanks. Unfortunately, the vertical armor plates of the Tiger I had been approved for production before the German invasion of the Soviet Union.

Despite its lack of well-sloped armor (when compared to the Soviet T-34 tank) the Tiger I, when introduced into service, featured the thickest armor ever fitted to a German tank: The front

vertical plate was 102 millimeters thick and the hull sides were 62 millimeters thick. Prior to the Tiger I introduction, the thickest armor plate found on a German tank was less than 50 millimeters. In an effort to further strengthen the Tiger I's various armor plates they were interlocked and step-jointed together.

The Tiger I's one-piece armored superstructure was a separate component that was welded to the hull during assembly. All earlier German tank designs had the armored superstructure bolted to the hull.

The turret of the Tiger I was made from a single, large piece of steel armor, 82 millimeters thick, bent into a horseshoe shape. At the front of the turret sat the Tiger I's 110-millimeter-thick mantle. (A mantle is the piece of armor that protects the gun mount in the front of the turret.) The turret could be turned manually by a handwheel, or by a hydraulic power traverse system controlled by the gunner.

The effectiveness of the thick armor on the Tiger I was reported in 1945 by Sergeant Harold E. Fulton, who described an engagement with a number of Tiger I tanks:

We were ordered to engage a column of six Mark VI's of the early model and two Mark IV's. As gunner, I fired 30 rounds from the 75-mm gun of our tank [M-4 Sherman medium tank]. Some were HE [high explosive], some smoke, and the rest AP [armor piecing]. Each time one of the AP's hit the tank you could see them ricocheting two and three hundred feet into the air. Along with my gun firing, there were four more tanks of my platoon. Two or three M-4 tanks from another company and two M-7's [self-propelled 105-mm howitzers] firing at the same column. The range from my tank to the targets was five to eight hundred yards.

Two days later, having a chance to inspect these vehicles, we found the Mark IV's with large holes in the front, but of all the Mark VI's there was one penetration in one tank on the back of the turret. The numerous places where the other projectiles hit there was just grooves or penetrations part way through the armor.

Shortly after World War II the Tiger I tank belonging to the U.S. Army Ordnance Museum had its left side opened for instructional purposes, as can clearly be seen in this picture. Current U.S. Army museum policy would not allow this type of mutilation of a historical artifact. When the sectionalized Tiger I was placed on outside display in the later 1960s, the museum staff welded sheet metal panels over the open sections of the vehicle's turret and hull to protect the interior of the vehicle from the elements. *Andreas Kirchhoff*

On display at the British Army Tank Museum is this Tiger II. The vehicle is the second prototype of the series with an early-style Krupp-designed turret. Fifty of these turrets were completed before production was switched to an improved model with thicker armor protection known as the series turret. *British Army Tank Museum*

In response to the fielding of the Tiger I, the Soviet army introduced new, more powerful, and larger weapons better able to punch holes in the thick skin of the Tiger I. This unpleasant development is reflected in an extract from a German army report in June 1944 that stated:

When Tigers first appeared on the battlefield, they were in every respect proof against enemy weapons. They quickly won for themselves the title of 'unbeatable' and 'undamageable.' But in the meantime, the enemy has not been asleep. A/Tk [antitank] guns, tanks and mines have been developed which can hit a Tiger hard and even knock it out. Now the Tiger, for a long time regarded as a 'Life Insurance Policy,' is relegated to the ranks of simply a 'heavy tank.'

On display at the Swiss Army Tank Museum is a Tiger II with a standard series turret. The large muzzle brake normally mounted on the end of the vehicle's long gun is missing from this vehicle. The 88-mm gun on the Tiger II was officially designated the Kwk 43. It had the highest performance in its size class during World War II. Similar weapons were under development in both England and the United States, but none of these reached active service during the war. *Andreas Kirchhoff*

The Tiger I suspension system consisted of front sprocket, rear idler, and large disc-type interleaved road wheels with independent torsion bar springing. The Germans first used interleaved road wheels during the 1930s on their early half-tracks. The extra road wheels found on the interleaved-type suspension system lowered a vehicle's ground pressure, a very important design consideration for any tank. It also meant the repair of any damage to an inner road wheel involved the time-consuming and difficult job of removing many outer road wheels first.

The Tiger I measured out at 20 feet 8 1/2 inches long (excluding gun), and 9 feet 4 3/4 inches tall. Due to shipping restrictions on European railroads, the Tiger I had two different sets of steel tracks for transport and combat. Tiger I was only 10 feet 4 inches wide during transport. The wider combat track gave the vehicle a width of 12 feet 3 inches. Tiger I was powered by a 12-cylinder Maybach engine that produced 700 horsepower in its final form. This gave the vehicle a top road speed of 25 miles per hour for short distances. Average road speed was around 15 miles per hour. Due to its heavy fuel consumption, the Tiger I had a maximum range of 90 miles on good roads, with a cross-country range of less than 50 miles. Unlike the mechanical transmissions found in earlier German tanks, the Tiger I had a Maybach-Olvar preselective gearbox, hydraulically operated with eight forward and four reverse gears.

TIGER II (TIGER B)

In May 1942, one month after the first prototypes of the Tiger I were shown to Hitler, the ordnance department of the German army authorized development of an improved Tiger tank originally designated as the Tiger H3. It would receive its more well-known title of Tiger II on March 16, 1943. The official German military designation for the Tiger II was Panzerkampfwagen Tiger Ausf. B. Its unofficial

Shown on display at the U.S. Army Ordnance Museum sometime in the late 1960s is a Tiger II tank still in its original colors. The vehicle was captured by American troops during the Battle of the Bulge in December 1944. Postwar research has indicated that at least 150 Tiger II tanks took part in Hitler's Ardennes counteroffensive. Many of these powerful vehicles were later found abandoned due to mechanical breakdowns or shortages of fuel. *Michael Green collection*

German nickname was the Koenigstiger (King Tiger). American and British soldiers would sometimes refer to the vehicle as the Tiger Royal or Royal Tiger.

The German ordnance department ordered 1,234 examples of the Tiger II from Henschel to be built in four different lots. At least 950 of them were to be completed by September 1945. But, the intense Allied bombing of German industry during the last two years of the war seriously disrupted the Tiger II production schedule. Henschel managed to complete only 477 examples of the vehicle between January 1944 and March 1945.

The Tiger II carried an improved 88-mm gun designated as the KwK 43. This weapon was 20 feet 8 inches long, making it the longest such weapon in World War II. It was capable of knocking out almost any vehicle within 1 1/2 miles. There was stowage space for up to 84 rounds in the Tiger II. Of those 84 rounds, 22 could be carried in the rear of the vehicle's turret, with the additional rounds stored in the hull. The armor-piercing rounds fired from the 88-mm gun on the Tiger II weighed almost 37 pounds each. A command version of the Tiger II, designated the Panzerbefehlswagen, carried only 63 rounds for the main gun due to the extra radio equipment installed in the vehicle.

The 68-ton Tiger II was the largest and heaviest tank to see action in World War II. It was 23 feet 10 inches long (excluding gun), 11 feet 11 1/2 inches wide, and 10 feet 2 inches tall.

In 1991 the Tiger II belonging to the collection of the U.S. Army Ordnance Museum was transferred to the Patton Museum of Cavalry and Armor. The Patton Museum staff decided, based on the resources available, that only a partial cosmetic restoration of the vehicle would be undertaken. This picture shows the Tiger II at Fort Knox, Kentucky, being towed by a U.S. Army M88A1 Armored Recovery Vehicle to a paint shop where it would be repainted in a scheme similar to the one it wore in World War II. *Dean and Nancy Kleffman*

In contrast to their design of the Tiger I, the Germans went to considerable effort to incorporate sloped armor plates into the design of the Tiger II. When the British army captured its first Tiger II in France in July 1944, the ordnance officers who looked it over noted the many design features it shared in common with the Panther tank, especially the sloping of the main armor plate. Despite some general outward similarities with the earlier Panther tank, the British ordnance officers warned in their evaluation report that "it would be a mistake to compare it with any previous German tank, as it mounted a gun with far superior performance to the gun in either the previous Tiger or Panther tanks and its armour affords a much greater degree of protection."

The steel armor on the front hull plate of the Tiger II was 150 millimeters thick, with the mantle being 185 millimeters thick. The two sides and rear of the turret were 80 millimeters thick. The turret roof on the Tiger II was 40 millimeters thick. The side and rear hull armor on the Tiger II was 80 millimeters thick.

Seen in this slightly washed-out picture is a Sturmmoerser Tiger at Aberdeen Proving Ground sometime shortly after World War II. The vehicle is pictured in its original wartime colors. Like all the vehicles that formed the basis of the U.S. Army Ordnance Museum collection, it would eventually be repainted with no regard for historical accuracy. Sometime in the 1960s the vehicle was loaned to the Wehrtechnische Studiensammlung (WTS) museum in Germany. *Charles Kliment collection*

Pictured on display at the British Army Tank Museum is one of only two examples built of a Jagdtiger with a Porsche-designed suspension system. Early testing soon showed the suspension system could not support the vehicle's 70-ton weight. The German army decided to stick with the standard Henschel-designed suspension system as fitted to the Tiger II. *British Army Tank Museum*

The effectiveness of the thick frontal armor on the King Tiger is described in a 1945 wartime report by Sergeant Clyde D. Brunson, a tank commander of the Second Armored Division:

One day a Tiger Royal (King Tiger) tank got within 150 yards of my tank and knocked me out. Five of our tanks opened up on him from ranges of 200 to 600 yards and got five or six hits on the front of the Tiger. They all just glanced off and the Tiger backed off and got away. If we had a tank like the Tiger, we would all be home today.

Even the thinner side armor on the Tiger II was effective against most U.S. Army tank guns.

Seen here in its current condition is the Jagdtiger belonging to the U.S. Army Ordnance Museum. The paint scheme is a vague duplication of what the vehicle wore when it first arrived at Aberdeen Proving Ground in 1945. The 70-ton Jagdtiger had a gasoline engine that could produce between 600 and 700 horsepower. This was the same engine mounted in late production examples of the Panther medium tanks that weighed only 45-tons, leaving the Jagdtiger badly underpowered. Traveling cross-country the vehicle had a top speed of only 9 miles per hour. *Michael Green*

Thomas H. Osborne, a first lieutenant in the American Second Armored Division, described an incident involving a Tiger II:

Plainly visible at 2,500 yards was a Mark VI with its side exposed to us. It was dug in up to the hull on a ridge commanding two draws. Another force was attempting to advance toward this vehicle and the enemy tank would hit two of ours, and the forces would withdraw. This continued for a day and a half, until the 'Kraut' ran out of ammunition and drove away. All during this time my platoon fired AP, smoke and HE, attempting to dislodge the enemy tank. We had at least 10 to 15 direct hits with 75-mm AP on the tank, but he failed to move, and we made no apparent impression on the vehicle's occupants.

The British army noted in its examination of the first captured example of a German Tiger II a minor change in the vehicle's suspension system. Rather than employing the interleaved road wheels found on the earlier Tiger I and Panther tanks, the Tiger II utilized an overlapping road wheel arrangement. This meant the vehicle's road wheels were placed alternately on the outside or inside of the tank's tracks. On

GERMAN VEHICLE PAINT SCHEMES

When the unprovoked German invasion of Poland began on September 1, 1939, officially beginning World War II, all German army vehicles (tracked and wheeled) were painted solid matte panzer gray. Panzer gray would remain the standard vehicle color for both the German army and the Waffen-SS until 1943. German air force vehicles wore a lighter shade of panzer gray. There was not a standard camouflage paint scheme until early 1943. Some units applied a dark green or brown striped pattern on top of the existing panzer gray to produce camouflage.

When the first German army units arrived in North Africa in early February 1941 to assist the Italian army, all vehicles were painted in a sand yellow color. However, some hurried late arrivals sent to North Africa were shipped in the standard panzer gray. To improve the camouflaging of their vehicles in North Africa, the Germans added matte gray-green lines. Eventually, the standard paint scheme on German vehicles in North Africa consisted of a dark brown base with a camouflage pattern of panzer gray.

Since German tankers considered painting to be a very low priority, German vehicles in North Africa often sported a wide mixture of colors based on whatever paint was available, including paint captured from enemy supply dumps.

In February 1943 the color standard was changed from panzer gray to matte dark yellow—called Dunkelgelb I. By 1943 the color was changed to the very similar Dunkelgelb II. All new or rebuilt vehicles delivered from the factory to German field units were painted Dunkelgelb yellow. Due to the difficulties German tank crews had repainting older vehicles in the field, many German vehicles were sloppily painted with visible strips or patterns of Dunkelgelb with the old panzer gray showing through.

For adding camouflage to the dark yellow base, German troops received cans of dark green and red-brown matte paints. The paints were delivered as a paste that needed to be thinned with gasoline or water. The preferred method was to use gasoline since the water-thinned paint was not as durable. The thinned paint could be applied with either a spray gun or brushes. Because of the many different types of thinning material used by German troops, including waste oil, the durability of the paint as well as the shades of color applied to their vehicles varied a great deal.

A very interesting variation in German tank colors was called the "Ambush" pattern. It consisted of alternating color spots applied to the vehicle's dark yellow base as well as the dark green and red-brown matte camouflage paints. The camouflage concept was designed to simulate lights and shadows normally generated by foliage, thereby allowing a German AFV to blend in with its background.

During the winter months the Germans often used white paint, whitewash, or chalk on their vehicles. Whitewash was an efficient coating for winter camouflage. The water-based paint tended to wash itself away with spring rains, assisted by the vehicle crew.

During the last few months of the war, paint was scarce, along with almost everything else. German factories often painted assembled vehicles in whatever colors were available before shipping them off to field units. This resulted in a wide variety of interesting schemes too numerous to list here.

the Tiger I and Panther tanks, each single alternate road wheel rotated between two other road wheels to its front and rear. This arrangement caused ice, rocks, and other obstructions to jam the track mechanism on many occasions. While the overlapping road wheel arrangement on the Tiger II was an improvement over the earlier interleaved system, it tended to place a potentially damaging, twisting load on tank tracks.

The biggest drawback with the interleaved and overlapping road wheel arrangements found on various German-track-laying vehicles during World War II was their design complexity and weight. No other country in World War II or in the postwar years adopted a similar system.

Despite its weight of almost 70 tons, the Tiger II was powered by the same 12-cylinder, 700 horsepower engine that propelled the 50-ton Panther medium tank, leaving it somewhat underpowered. This weight strained almost all the powertrain components of the vehicle, including the steering mechanism and hydraulically operated transmission.

The Tiger II had a top speed of 26 miles per hour and a maximum range on good roads of about 100 miles. Cross-country operational range of the Tiger II was less than 50 miles.

In spite of their size, weight, and low power, the Tiger tanks were more mobile in many types of terrain than most of the smaller and lighter Allied tanks. Captain Henry W. Johnson of the U.S. Army's Second Armored Division stated in a wartime report:

> The wider tracks of the Mark V and the Mark VI enables it to move much better cross-country and in muddy or snow-covered terrain, than the narrow tracks of the Sherman tank. The field expedient of duckbills [track extensions] added to widen the Sherman tread aids, but does not effect the advantage the German Mark V and Mark VI tanks have. It is my opinion that the Mark V and Mark VI enemy tank is far superior in maneuverability to our Sherman tanks.

SELECTED TIGER VARIANTS

The small number of Tiger tanks built between 1942 and 1945 resulted in far fewer variants than those based on the chassis of German light and medium tanks.

One of the few Tiger variants was based on German combat experience in Soviet cities and the need for a very large close-range assault weapon. The gun had to be powerful enough to destroy an enemy-held multi-story brick or concrete building with a single round. To meet this need, Alkett adapted a large naval high-explosive depth charge (716 pounds) into a rocket-assisted projectile to be fired from a short-barreled breech-loaded mortar. This unique weapon system was grafted onto the chassis of a handful of Tiger I tanks between August and December 1943. Eighteen of the 65-ton vehicles (designated Sturmmoerser Tiger) were produced. The official German military designation for the Sturmmoerser was 38-cm RW61 auf Stu Mrs Tiger.

A large, box-like armored superstructure on the front of the chassis housed the limited-traverse mortar and ammunition. Twelve rounds were carried inside the superstructure of the Sturmmoerser. To assist the seven-man crew in reloading the vehicle, a small hand-operated crane was fitted to the rear of the vehicle's superstructure.

The weapon system was used at relatively close range, so the frontal armor was up to 150 millimeters thick, and the front glacis was steeply angled. The rocket-assisted projectiles could be fired either in direct or indirect fire mode.

By the time the Sturmmoerser Tigers reached field units, the need for this specialized weapon system had vanished. The Sturmmoerser is yet another example of failed development efforts indulged in by the Germans toward the end of World War II.

Another specialized vehicle failure built on a Tiger tank chassis was the massive 70-ton Jagdtiger. The first prototype showed up in April 1944. It was armed with one of two types

Pictured at Aberdeen Proving Ground shortly after World War II is this side view of a Jagdtiger in its original wartime colors. Visible is the large, sloping, box-like armored superstructure that housed the vehicle's 128-mm gun and its four-man gun crew. The Jagdtiger carried 38 main gun rounds, and 2,925 rounds of 7.92-mm ammunition for its two machine guns. The armor-piercing rounds fired by the Jagdtiger weighed 62.4 pounds each. *Charles Kliment collection*

of 128-mm guns. The weapon was originally developed as an antiaircraft gun. Like other wartime German Jagdpanzers, the gun was mounted in a limited-traverse mount. The official German designation for the Jagdtiger was Panzerkampfwagen Jaeg Tiger Auf. B.

The Jagdtiger was based on a King Tiger tank chassis that was lengthened by 10 inches. The 128-mm gun was mounted in a large, sloped, armored box-like superstructure. The frontal armor was 250 millimeters thick. Excluding the gun, the vehicle was 23 feet 10 inches long, 11 feet 9 1/2 inches wide, and 9 feet 3 inches tall. Including the gun, the Jagdtiger was 32 feet 2 inches long.

The six-man gun crew included a vehicle commander, gunner, and two loaders who occupied the heavily armored superstructure, and a driver and hull machine gunner/radio operator located in the front of the hull.

The ordnance department of the German army set the requirements for the Jagdtiger in early 1943, with an initial order of 150 vehicles. The German firm of Nibelungenwerke finished the first vehicle in July 1944. Only 40 to 70 vehicles were produced before Germany surrendered. It is estimated that fewer than half actually saw combat. A number of Jagdtigers were armed with the same 88-mm gun mounted in the Jagdpanther when the standard 128-mm gun was not available.

four

TANK SUPPORT VEHICLES

✦ ✦ ✦

The German army Panzertruppen were never just an all-tank force. Without the support of infantry, artillery, antitank, engineers, reconnaissance, and communications units, tank formations are unable to hold ground once conquered. As part of a well-trained combined-arms team, German tanks were extremely effective in combat. During the first few years of World War II, German ground attack aircraft also played an important role in the successes enjoyed by the Panzertruppen.

ARMORED HALF-TRACKS

A number of specialized vehicles were developed to provide a reasonable amount of mobility to the non-tank units of panzer divisions. One of the best known specialized vehicles was an armored half-track designated the Mittlerer (medium) Schutzenpanzerwagen (infantry-tank-vehicle) or just Sd.Kfz 251. The designation *Sd.Kfz* indicated a special-purpose army vehicle. The numbers that followed gave the vehicle's ordnance number.

This nicely restored unarmored German half-track belongs to the collection of the Patton Museum of Cavalry and Armor. The vehicle pictured was designed to have a payload carrying capacity of 1 ton. Normally, it was used to tow equipment, like small anti-aircraft or antitank guns. The gun crews sat on bench seats within the vehicle. *Michael Green*

The Sd.Kfz 251 first appeared in German army service in 1939. By the end of the war, German industry had built over 15,252 Sd.Kfz 251s. The Sd.Kfz 251 series of half-tracks came in four basic versions (Ausf. A through Ausf. D). These four basic models were the basis for over 22 different official variants, ranging from anti-aircraft to engineering support vehicles. All versions were powered by a six-cylinder Maybach gasoline engine. The vehicle had a top road speed of 32.5 miles per hour and a maximum range of 186 miles. It was 19 feet 3 inches long, 6 feet 10.7 inches wide, and 5 feet 8.9 inches tall.

The Sd.Kfz 251 was based on the chassis of an unarmored 3-ton half-track originally designed to tow artillery pieces. In its most common configuration, the open-topped Sd.Kfz 251 carried a crew of two (a vehicle commander and a driver) and 10 infantrymen known as Panzergrenadiers (armored infantry). In addition to the weapons carried by its onboard infantry, the vehicle normally mounted two 7.92-mm machine guns for self-protection. Due to its light armor protection of only 6- to 14.5-millimeter-thick armor steel, the Sd.Kfz 251 was very vulnerable to enemy fire and had to be employed very carefully to avoid high losses.

The U.S. Army first encountered the Sd.Kfz 251 series of half-tracks in Tunisia in late 1943. American opinion on the vehicle's worth was mixed. An officer of the U.S. Army's 17th Armored Engineer Battalion compared

On display at the British Army Tank Museum is a Sd.Kfz 251 Ausf. C painted in a panzer gray by the museum staff. The vehicle is actually an ambulance version of the Sd.Kfz 251 series captured in North Africa by the British army. As an armored ambulance, the vehicle was designed to carry two stretcher cases and four seated wounded passengers. This vehicle was constructed with riveted armor plates. *British Army Tank Museum*

American and German armored half-tracks in a wartime report:

> It is the general opinion that the U.S. half-track on the whole is far superior to the German half-track. The lack of front-wheel drive reduces tractive power and makes the vehicle extremely difficult to turn in soft ground. It has been found that the German half-track throws its tracks easily on sharp turns and is inferior to our own in this respect.

UNARMORED HALF-TRACKS AND VARIANTS

The German army developed a selection of Zugkraftwagens (unarmored half-track towing vehicles), originally divided into light, medium, and heavy classes. The unarmored half-tracks were later classified by the load they could carry or tow. The former light class had three different vehicles designated as the 1-ton, 3-ton, and 5-ton. The former medium class had a single 8-ton vehicle. The former heavy class had a 12-ton and an 18-ton vehicle.

Seen on outdoor display at the Patton Museum of Cavalry and Armor in the 1970s is this Sd.Kfz 251 Ausf. D configured as an engineering vehicle. In the 1980s all the German World War II vehicles on outdoor display were placed into storage to protect them from the elements. The vehicle was transferred to the German Army Tank Museum in the 1980s. *Dean and Nancy Kleffman*

Taking part in a display of military vehicles organized by the German Army Tank Museum is a Sd.Kfz 251 Ausf. D configured as an engineering vehicle. General Patton's famous Third Army captured the vehicle in World War II. It was shipped back to Fort Knox, Kentucky, home of the U.S. Army Armor School, as a war trophy and later formed the basis of the Patton Museum of Cavalry and Armor. In the 1980s it was transferred to the German Army Tank Museum and restored with a late-war camouflage scheme. *Thomas Anderson*

A 4.9-ton unarmored half-track with a 1-ton carrying capacity first appeared in German army service in 1934. Over 17,000 examples of the vehicle were built during the war years. The vehicle was 15 feet 7 inches long, 6 feet wide, and 5 feet 4 inches high. Its main role was to tow a variety of light antitank or antiaircraft guns. Power came from a Maybach gasoline engine that yielded a top speed of 25 miles per hour. The vehicle carried a crew of eight men situated on simple bench seats.

The same 4.9-ton half-track chassis formed the basis for a small armored reconnaissance

On display at a British military collector's show in the summer of 1999 is Mike Gibb's newly restored German military Sd.Kfz 250 armored half-track. The Sd.Kfz 250 series was a smaller version of the Sd.Kfz 251 series of armored half-tracks, and first saw action during the invasion of France in May 1940. Configured as an armored personnel carrier, the vehicle had a crew of six men and was armed with two 7.92-mm machine guns. *Panzer Prints*

half-track designated the Schutzenpanzerwagen Sd.Kfz 250. Like the larger Sd.Kfz 251, the Sd.Kfz 250 eventually served in a wide variety of roles. German industry would build 4,250 Sd.Kfz 250s between June 1941 and October 1943.

The 18-ton (load capacity) unarmored German half-track coincidentally weighed 18 tons. It had a crew of nine and was 27 feet long, 8 feet 6 inches wide, and 9 feet 1 inch tall. The first production model entered the German army inventory in 1938. It would see service in a variety of roles including tank recovery vehicle, artillery-towing vehicle, and as a portable bridge-towing vehicle attached to German army engineering units. German industry would produce about 300 of these vehicles before the war ended.

To improve the cross-country mobility of military trucks, German industry converted a number of wheeled vehicles from different manufacturers into half-track trucks, called Maultiers (Mules). This modification replaced the vehicle's rear axle and wheels with a tracked module. Many of these half-track trucks featured the suspension components from the Panzer II light tank. The first of these vehicles appeared in late 1942. Production ended in 1944 with a total of 4,000 Maultiers produced.

The usefulness of the Maultier concept convinced the German army to produce an armored variant weighing 7.1 tons in 1942. The official designation was the 15-cm Panzerwerfer 42 auf Sf (Sd.Kfz 4/1), of which 300 were built by the time production ended in March 1944.

The armored version of the Maultier carried a 10-barrel Nebelwerfer (rocket launcher) on its rear superstructure. The rocket launcher, consisting of two horizontal rows of five barrels, was mounted on a turntable with 360-degree traverse. The high-explosive rockets fired from the launcher unit weighed 78 pounds and had a maximum range of 7,330 yards. The rockets were fired electrically by a gunner who sat inside the vehicle.

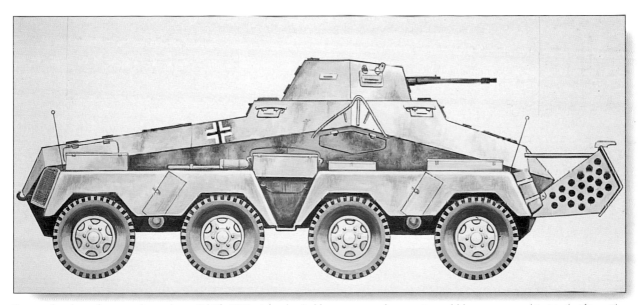

Depicted in this color artwork is a large Sd.Kfz 231 eight-wheeled heavy armored car as it would have appeared in North Africa. The vehicle was armed with a single turret-mounted 20-mm gun. In comparison with many foreign armored cars in the early-war period, the Sd.Kfz 231 was undergunned. This reflected the German belief that armored cars were not really designed to fight but were to concentrate on their main mission of seeking out information on enemy dispositions. *George Bradford*

ARMORED CARS

In the late 1920s, the German army began development work on its first generation of post–World War I Panzerspaehwagens (armored cars). Standard German army practice was to dispatch three armored cars on a reconnaissance patrol. The patrols would normally last from one to two days. At least one of the armored cars would be equipped with a powerful radio. The Germans would also send an artillery observer along with the patrols to call in emergency fire when required.

The primary job of German armored cars assigned to reconnaissance missions was to seek out information on enemy troop dispositions and pass it on to higher commands. If an enemy force was met during the conduct of such patrols, action was to be avoided at all costs unless the enemy force was so weak that it could be destroyed without diverting the patrol from its main job. If the Germans anticipated that

their reconnaissance patrols would meet enemy resistance, they would be reinforced with self-propelled assault guns and occasionally with tanks. Engineers and motorcyclists could also be attached to reconnaissance patrol to deal with roadblocks or minefields.

The first armored car to be fielded was the six-wheeled, 5.7-ton Sd.Kfz. 231 (6-Rad) armored car. (In German army nomenclature, any vehicle with more than four wheels was distinguished by the inclusion of the words "6-Rad" or "8-Rad," indicating a six- or eight-wheeled vehicle.) It was 15 feet 9 inches long, 6 feet 5 inches wide, and 5 feet 7 inches tall. Between 1932 and 1937, 151 vehicles were produced. The vehicle was based on the chassis of a commercial truck and was operated by a crew of four. The engine was at the front of the vehicle. The main armament consisted of a turret-mounted 20-mm gun. The secondary armament was a coaxial 7.92-mm machine gun. The Sd.Kfz 231 (6-Rad) saw service during the invasions of both Poland and France. Due to its poor cross-country mobility, it was restricted only to training duties after 1940.

The replacement for the Sd.Kfz 231 (6-Rad) was the purpose-built Sd.Kfz 231 (8-Rad). Like its predecessor, it had a four-man crew. Development of the vehicle began in 1935, and the first production vehicle was turned over to the German army in 1937. The Sd.Kfz 231 (8-Rad) was 19 feet 2 inches long, 7 feet 2 1/2 inches wide, and 7 feet 8 inches high. The Maybach gasoline engine was located at the rear of the vehicle.

At the time of its fielding, the 8.3-ton Sd.Kfz 231 (8-Rad) was the most advanced cross-country vehicle in worldwide military service. It incorporated all-wheel drive and steering, and front and rear driving controls. The initial version of the Sd.Kfz 231 (8-Rad) was armed with a turret-mounted 20-mm gun and a coaxial 7.92-mm machine gun. The command variant was designated Sd.Kfz 263 (8-Rad).

The German army also fielded a fire-support vehicle armed with a limited-traverse 75-mm howitzer designated Sd.Kfz 233 (8-Rad). Due to

Pictured on outdoor display at the Patton Museum of Cavalry and Armor sometime in the 1970s is a radio communication version of the standard Sd.Kfz 221 armored car. The vehicle has no turret or weapons. The only weapons were the four-man crew's personal firearms. This vehicle was removed from outdoor display in the 1980s and placed into interior storage to protect it from the elements. *Dean and Nancy Kleffman*

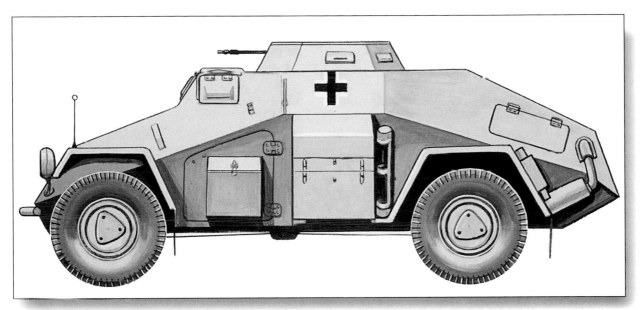

Depicted in this color artwork is a small four-wheeled Sd.Kfz 221 armored car as it would have appeared in North Africa. This two-man vehicle was armed only with a single turret-mounted 7.92-mm machine gun. A rear-mounted gasoline engine gave the Sd.Kfz 221 armored car a top speed of 50 miles per hour. Traveling cross-country dropped the vehicle's speed down to 25 miles per hour. *George Bradford*

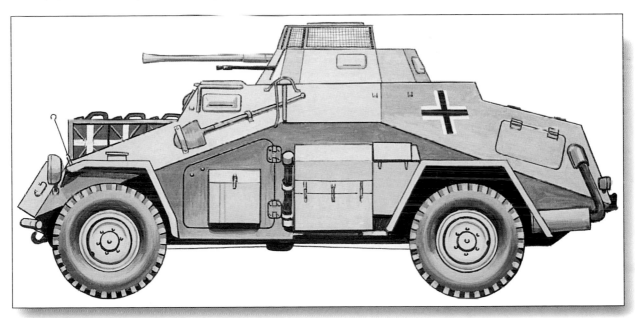

An improved version of the Sd.Kfz 221 was the Sd.Kfz 222, which featured a larger open-topped turret armed with a 20-mm gun and a coaxial 7.92-mm machine gun. The turret-mounted 20-mm gun could be raised vertically in an antiaircraft role. The vehicle also featured heavier armor protection on its front than its earlier cousin, the Sd.Kfz 221. The vehicle is depicted in the sand color paint scheme worn by German vehicles serving in North Africa. Production of the Sd.Kfz 222 ended in 1943. *George Bradford*

the size of the howitzer, it was fitted in an open mount on the top of the vehicle's superstructure. Total production was 976 vehicles, starting in 1936 and ending in 1943.

Combat experience gained during the invasions of Poland and France identified several important performance deficiencies in German eight-wheeled armored cars. In response, an eight-wheel improvement program based on a new set of requirements began in August of 1940. The outcome was the slightly larger and heavier eight-wheeled armored car series designated Sd.Kfz 234 (8-Rad). The new versions were 19 feet 9 inches long, 7 feet 9 inches wide, and 6 feet 10 inches high.

Major features of the Sd.Kfz 234 (8-Rad) series included Czech-built diesel engines, one-piece hulls, better armor protection, and large

Pictured on outdoor display at the Patton Museum of Cavalry and Armor sometime in the 1970s is this large eight-wheeled armored car equipped with a 75-mm gun. In this configuration the vehicle was designated the Sd.Kfz 234/4. Its development reflected a late-war policy by the German army to place a tank-killing weapon on almost any vehicle that could carry one. In the 1980s the Sd.Kfz 234/4 was placed into interior storage to protect it from the elements. *Dean and Nancy Kleffman*

low-pressure tires. These huge tires gave the vehicle superior cross-country mobility compared to the earlier generation of German eight-wheeled armored cars.

Each of the four different versions of the redesigned eight-wheeled armored car featured a different armament: The Sd.Kfz 234/1, of which 200 were built, had an open-topped turret fitted with a 20-mm gun and a coaxial 7.92-mm machine gun. The Sd.Kfz 234/2, officially nicknamed the Puma (Cougar), featured a fully enclosed turret armed with a 50-mm gun and a coaxial 7.92-mm machine gun. (Only 101 examples of the Puma were built between September of 1943 and September of 1944.) The Sd.Kfz 234/3 had a 75-mm howitzer mounted in an open-topped, limited-traverse mount. In late 1944 Hitler ordered the 234/3 vehicle up-gunned to a 75-mm gun. In its new configuration the vehicle was designated Sd.Kfz 234/4, of which only 89 were built, between December 1944 and March 1945.

The German army also fielded a light four-wheeled armored car. This vehicle, designated Kfz 13, was a makeshift vehicle based on the chassis of a four-wheel-drive passenger car. This simple open-topped 2.1-ton vehicle with a two-man crew and front engine first appeared in 1932. Production would end in 1934 with a total production run of 147 vehicles. It was 13 feet 9 inches long, 5 feet 7 inches wide, and 4 feet 11 inches high.

The command variant was a three-man vehicle designated Kfz 14. Both versions saw service during the invasion of Poland in September 1939. A mere handful would serve in the invasion of France in May 1940 before being pulled from service.

The replacement for the Kfz 13 and 14 was the four-wheeled armored car designated the Sd.Kfz 221, which was based on the chassis of an existing rear-engine, German four-wheel-drive passenger car. The Sd.Kfz weighed 4 tons and had a crew of two men. It was 15 feet 9 inches long, 6 feet 5 inches wide, and 5 feet 7 inches high.

Armament consisted of a single 7.92-mm machine gun in an open-topped turret. Another version, designated Sd.Kfz 222, carried a

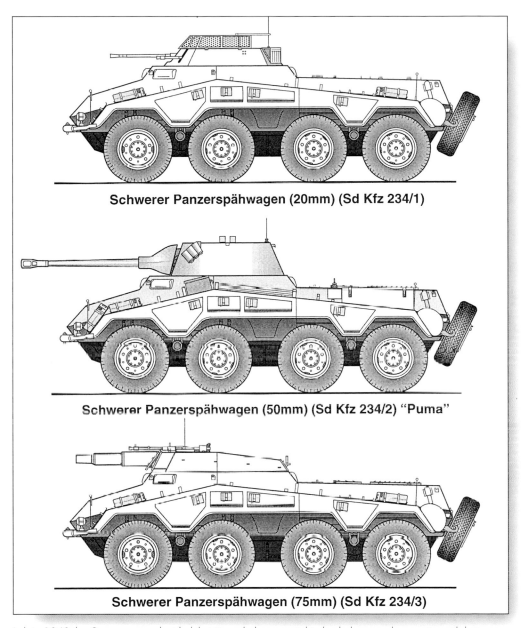

Schwerer Panzerspähwagen (20mm) (Sd Kfz 234/1)

Schwerer Panzerspähwagen (50mm) (Sd Kfz 234/2) "Puma"

Schwerer Panzerspähwagen (75mm) (Sd Kfz 234/3)

In late 1940 the German army decided that it needed a new eight-wheeled armored car series with better mobility and armor protection. The first three vehicles in that new series of eight-wheeled armored cars are depicted in these line drawings. The first vehicle ordered in the series was the Sd.Kfz 234/2 Puma (Cougar) armed with a turret-mounted 50-mm gun (middle). The first to enter service was the Sd.Kfz 234/1 armed with an open-topped turret with a 20-mm gun and a 7.92-mm coaxial machine gun (top). The third version in the series to enter production was the Sd.Kfz 234/3 armed with a 75-mm howitzer in an open-topped superstructure (bottom). *George Bradford*

Pictured on display at the French Army Tank Museum is this beautifully restored German Maultier (Mule). Clearly visible is the ten-barreled rocket launcher mounted on the vehicle's rear deck. The mounting of the rocket launcher unit on an armored half-track was done to improve the weapon system's overall mobility, since once fired it tended to attract enemy counter battery fire. *Ground Power Magazine*

Pictured on display at the British Army Tank Museum is this large eight-wheeled heavy armored car armed with a 75-mm howitzer in an open-topped superstructure. In this configuration the vehicle was designated as the Sd.Kfz 233 and was used to support its lighter armored cousins during reconnaissance missions. The vehicle was painted in this early-war panzer gray by the museum staff. *British Army Tank Museum*

turret-mounted 20-mm gun and a coaxial 7.92-mm machine gun. The Sd.Kfz 222 turret was also open-topped. A two-part wire mesh screen over the open top prevented hand grenades from entering the vehicle. Three different unarmed radio vehicles, designated Sd.Kfz 260, 261, and 223, completed the series. Total production of these light armored cars was 2,370 units between 1935 and early 1944.

The German army supported its panzer divisions with a wide variety of non-armored wheeled vehicles. The best-known example is the small rear-engine Volkswagen Kubel (bucket). First produced in 1940 and known as the Kubelwagen, it was the standard light passenger car of the German armed forces (Wehrmacht). The vehicle was 12 feet

Pictured is a fully restored Type 82 Volkswagen Kubel (bucket) better known to most people as the Kubelwagen. Unlike the even-better-known, American-designed and -built four-wheel-drive Jeep, only the rear wheels were driven on the Kubelwagen. To assist the vehicle's off-road mobility it had a reduction gear mounted on the ends of the rear axle shafts. Still, the vehicle could never match the off-road ability of the American Jeep. *Richard Pemberton*

Pictured during a display of German military vehicles is this Krupp-designed light truck commonly called the "Boxer." It was the most common truck in German army service during the 1930s. Power for the vehicle came from an air-cooled four-cylinder engine. The most common role of the Boxer was as a towing vehicle for light antitank guns or infantry support howitzers. Of the vehicle's six wheels, only four were driven. *Thomas Anderson*

3 inches long, 5 feet 3 inches wide, and 5 feet 5 inches tall.

The German Kubelwagen did not compare well with the better-known American wartime Jeep. Its four-cylinder gasoline air-cooled engine was low in power and performance. Instead of having four-wheel drive, as found on the American Jeep, the Kubelwagen had only two-wheel drive. With a very low center of gravity, the low-slung German vehicle also proved unable to travel over extremely rough or rocky terrain, something in which the American Jeep performed very well.

German industry would build about 55,000 of the simple and inexpensive Kubelwagens before production ceased in mid-1944. The two standard versions were the Type 82 followed by the slightly larger Type 86. The most interesting variant of the Kubelwagen was an amphibious version known as the Schwimmwagen that first entered Ger-

man army service in 1942. Production of the vehicle ended in 1944 after 14,265 units had been produced.

The German army was short of trucks throughout World War II. This forced them to field many different types of commercial vehicles, including some of foreign manufacture. The commercial vehicles were unable to stand the strain of hard military use and were no match for American or German trucks built specifically for military service.

German industry's inability to design or build a suitable fleet of wheeled military support vehicles stands in sharp contrast to its ability to develop some of the most powerful and deadly tanks to see action during World War II. The opposite was true of American industry, which managed to design and build an outstanding selection of wheeled military vehicles, but could not produce a first-rate tank until the very closing stages of World War II.

SELECTED BIBLIOGRAPHY

✦ ✦ ✦

Doyle, Hilary & Thomas L. Jentz. *StuG III, Assault Gun, 1940–1942*. London: Osprey, 1996.

Chamberlain, Peter; Hilary Doyle; and Thomas L. Jentz. *Encyclopedia of German Tanks of World War Two*. London: Arms and Armour Press, 1978.

Cooper, Matthew. *The German Army 1933–1945*. London: Scarborough House, 1978.

Crow, Duncan, ed. *AFVs of Germany*. London: Barrie & Jenkins, 1973.

Culver, Bruce. *The SdKfz 251 Half-Track*. London: Osprey/Vanguard, 1983.

Culver, Bruce, and Uwe Feist. *Schutzenpanzer*. Bellingham, WA: Ryton Publications, 1997.

Forty, George. *German Tanks of World War II*. London: Arms and Armour Press, 1988.

Jentz, Thomas L. *Panzer Truppen*. Atglen, PA: Schiffer, 1996.

Jentz, Thomas L. *Germany's Panther Tank: The Quest For Combat Supremacy*. Atglen, PA: Schiffer, 1995.

Jentz, Thomas L. & Hilary Doyle. *Tiger I, Heavy Tank 1942–1945*. London: Osprey, 1993.

Jentz, Thomas L. & Hilary Doyle. *Kingtiger, Heavy Tank 1942–1945*. London: Osprey, 1993.

Jentz, Thomas L. & Hilary Doyle. *Germany Tiger Tanks, VK45.02 to Tiger II: Design, Production & Modifications*. Atglen, PA: Schiffer, 1993.

Kliment, Charles, and Vladimir Francev. *Czechoslovak Armored Fighting Vehicles 1918–1948*. Atglen, PA: Schiffer. 1997.

Macksey, Kenneth J. *Tank Warfare: A History of Tanks in Battle*. London: Hart-Davis, 1971.

———. *Guderian: Panzer General*. London: Macdonald & Jane's, 1975.

———, and John H. Batchelor. *Tank: A History of the Armoured Fighting Vehicle*. London: Macdonald, 1975.

Perrett, Bryan. *Knights of the Black Cross*. New York: St. Martin Press, 1986.

———. *The PzKpfw V Panther*. London: Osprey/Vanguard, 1981.

———. *German Light Panzers 1932–1942*. London: Osprey/Vanguard, 1983.

Rieger, Kurt, and Uwe Feist. *Militarfahrzeuge of the Wehrmacht*. Bellingham, WA: Ryton Publications, 1997.

Spielberger, W.J. *Panzer IV & Its Variants*. Atglen, PA: Schiffer, 1993.

———. *Panzer III & Variants*. Atglen, PA: Schiffer, 1993.

———. *Sturmgeschuetz & Its Variants*. Atglen, PA: Schiffer, 1993.

War Department U.S. Handbook on German Military Forces (Technical Manual TM-E 30-451). Washington, D.C.: Govt. Printing Office, 1945.

Windrow, Martin. *The Panzer Division*. London: Osprey, 1973.

INDEX

✦ ✦ ✦